GRADE
5

Writing everyday

Intervention Acti

D1536712

Table of Contents

Using Everyday Writing Intervention Activities

Research shows that reading and writing are reciprocal processes, and often the same students who struggle as readers need support to develop their writing skills.

The Everyday Writing Intervention Activities Series provides developmentally appropriate, easy-to-use, five-day writing units for Grades K–5. Each unit focuses on a particular writing process or writer's craft skill and provides multiple opportunities for students to practice that skill. As students complete these engaging mini-lessons, they will build a repertoire of writing skills they can apply as they write independently during writer's workshop, respond to texts they have read, complete content-area writing assignments, or write to prompts on standardized assessments.

These units are structured around a research-based model-guide-practice-apply approach. You can use these activities in a variety of intervention models, including Response to Intervention (RTI).

Getting Started

In just five simple steps, Everyday Writing Intervention Activities provides everything you need to identify students' needs and to provide targeted intervention.

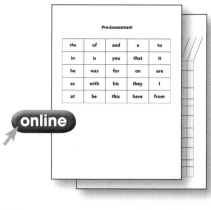

1. PRE-ASSESS to identify students' writing needs. Use the pre-assessment to identify the skills your students need to master.

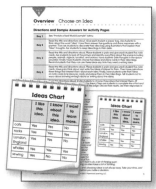

2. MODEL the skill.
Every five-day unit targets a specific writing study area. On Day 1, use the teacher prompts and reproducible activity page to introduce and model the skill.

Day 1

3. GUIDE, PRACTICE, and APPLY.
Use the reproducible practice activities for Days 2, 3, and 4 to build students' understanding and skill proficiency.

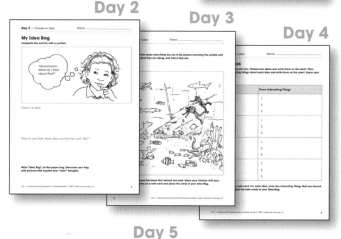

Day 2

Day 3

Day 4

Day 5

4. MONITOR progress.
Administer the Day 5 reproducible assessment to monitor each student's progress and to make instructional decisions.

5. POST-ASSESS to document student progress.
Use the post-assessment to measure students' progress as a result of your interventions.

Standards-Based Writing Awareness & Writing Skills in Everyday Intervention Activities

The writing strategies found in the Everyday Intervention Activities series are introduced developmentally and spiral from one grade to the next. The chart below shows the types of words and skill areas addressed at each grade level in this series.

Everyday Writing Intervention Activities Series Skills	K	1	2	3	4	5
Choosing a topic	✔	✔	✔	✔	✔	✔
Narrow the focus	✔	✔	✔	✔	✔	✔
Develop the idea (list what I know, research, complete list)	✔	✔	✔	✔	✔	✔
Organizing ideas/Writing an outline	✔	✔	✔	✔	✔	✔
Strong leads (fiction)	✔	✔	✔	✔	✔	✔
Strong leads (nonfiction)	✔	✔	✔	✔	✔	✔
Developing a character	✔	✔	✔	✔	✔	✔
Developing a plot	✔	✔	✔	✔	✔	✔
Strong endings (fiction)	✔	✔	✔	✔	✔	✔
Strong endings (nonfiction)	✔	✔	✔	✔	✔	✔
What is voice?	✔	✔	✔	✔	✔	✔
How do I write in my voice?	✔	✔	✔	✔	✔	✔
Different voices	✔	✔	✔	✔	✔	✔
Adjectives	✔	✔	✔	✔	✔	✔
Adverbs	✔	✔	✔	✔	✔	✔
Verbs	✔	✔	✔	✔	✔	✔
Nouns	✔	✔	✔	✔		
Advanced nouns					✔	✔
Idioms			✔	✔	✔	✔
Similes			✔	✔	✔	✔
Metaphors					✔	✔
Personification						✔

Using Everyday Intervention for RTI

According to the National Center on Response to Intervention, RTI "integrates assessment and intervention within a multi-level prevention system to maximize student achievement and to reduce behavior problems." This model of instruction and assessment allows schools to identify at-risk students, monitor their progress, provide research-proven interventions, and "adjust the intensity and nature of those interventions depending on a student's responsiveness."

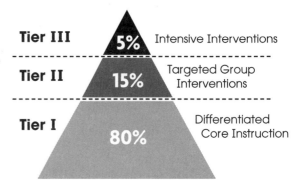

RTI models vary from district to district, but the most prevalent model is a three-tiered approach to instruction and assessment.

The Three Tiers of RTI	Using Everyday Intervention Activities
Tier I: Differentiated Core Instruction • Designed for all students • Preventive, proactive, standards-aligned instruction • Whole- and small-group differentiated instruction • Daily literacy instruction	• Use whole-group writing mini-lessons to introduce and guide practice with writing strategies that all students need to learn. • Use any or all of the units in the order that supports your core instructional program.
Tier II: Targeted Group Interventions • For struggling readers and writers • Provide thirty minutes of daily instruction beyond the Tier I core literacy instruction • Instruction is conducted in small groups of three to five students with similar needs	• Select units based on your students' areas of need (the pre-assessment can help you identify these). • Use the units as week-long, small-group mini-lessons.
Tier III: Intensive Interventions • For high-risk students experiencing considerable difficulty in reading and writing • Provide up to sixty minutes of additional intensive intervention each day in addition to the ninety-minute Tier I core reading instruction • More intense and explicit instruction • Instruction conducted individually or with smaller groups of one to three students with similar needs	• Select units based on your students' areas of need. • Use the units as one component of an intensive reading and writing intervention program.

Overview   Choose an Idea

Directions and Sample Answers for Activity Pages

Day 1	See "Provide a Real-World Example" below.
Day 2	Read the title and directions aloud. Give each student a paper bag. Ask students to think about the word "idea." Have them answer the questions and share responses with a partner. Then ask students to decorate their idea bag using illustrations that explain their "idea" thoughts. Ask students to keep Idea Bags in their desks.
Day 3	Read the title and directions aloud. Place students in pairs and give each student five note cards. Ask students to look at the picture and identify everything about the scene including people, animals, objects, location, and actions. Have students write thoughts in the space provided. Finally, have students choose five ideas and place cards in their Idea Bags. Remind students that they can use these ideas any time they need a writing idea.
Day 4	Read the title and directions aloud. Place students in pairs and give each student four note cards. Have pairs think about and write four ideas of interest to them. Then have pairs share three things that interest them about each idea. Finally, have students write their ideas on note cards (one idea per card), and place them in their Idea Bags. Tell students not to worry about knowing enough about or writing about the ideas.
Day 5	Read the directions aloud. Invite students to choose three ideas that interest them. (If students struggle, provide examples for them.) Then ask students to complete the chart and answer the questions at the bottom of the page. Discuss their results. Use their responses to plan further instruction.

Provide a Real-World Example

◆ **Say:** *One of the hardest things writers do is choose an idea to write about. Sometimes, the things that you think about are often the best ideas to write about. There are three important things to remember about choosing a writing idea. Choose an idea that interests you. Choose an idea that you know something about. Choose an idea you want to learn more about.*

◆ Hand out Day 1 activity. **Say:** *Look at the chart. I wrote five things that interest me, but I don't really want to write about all of them. Watch as I choose a writing idea that works for me. I like cats, and I know a little bit about them. But I really don't want to learn more right now.* Place a Yes and No in the appropriate columns.

◆ **Say:** *I love rocks and know quite a bit about them. I'm very interested in the rock cycle. (Use the completed chart to continue the process.) It looks like I am most interested in writing about rocks and whales. Now I just need to decide between the two. Whales are really cool. I could write about different kinds of whales. I'd need to do some research. Rocks are cool, too. There are so many*

Ideas Chart

Idea	I like this idea.	I know about this idea.	I want to learn more.
cats	Yes	Yes	No
rocks	Yes	Yes	Yes
London, England	Yes	Yes	No
whales	Yes	Yes	Yes
sewing	Yes	No	No

different kinds of rocks, and they can be used for so many things. The research might be kind of fun. I think I like rocks better than whales. Wow! I had to do a lot of thinking even when I narrowed it down to two ideas. I guess choosing an idea takes a lot of thinking.

◆ **Say:** *Remember, all writers choose ideas, and choosing ideas is not always easy. Take your time, and think about what you like and don't like before you make a decision.*

Name _____

Choose an Idea

Complete the chart.

Ideas Chart

Idea	I like this idea.	I know about this idea.	I want to learn more.
cats			
rocks			
London, England			
whales			
sewing			

My Idea Bag

Complete the activity with a partner.

What is an idea?

What do you think about when you hear the word "idea"?

**Write "Idea Bag" on the paper bag. Decorate your bag
with pictures that explain your "idea" thoughts.**

Picture This

Look at the picture. Write down everything you see in the picture including the people and things around them, what they are doing, and where they are.

Read your ideas. Choose five ideas that interest you most. Share your choices with your partner. Write each idea on a note card and place the cards in your Idea Bag.

 Unit 1 • Everyday Writing Intervention Activities Grade 5 • ©2011 Newmark Learning, LLC

Writing Ideas

**Think about what interests you. Choose four ideas and write them
on the chart. Then identify three interesting things about each idea and
write them on the chart. Share your ideas with a partner.**

Ideas Chart

Idea	Three Interesting Things
	1. 2. 3.
	1. 2. 3.
	1. 2. 3.
	1. 2. 3.

**Write each idea on a note card. For each idea, write two interesting things
that you shared with your partner. Place the note cards in your Idea Bag.**

Assessment

Look at the chart. In the left-hand column write three ideas that interest you. Then complete the chart with Yes or No.

Ideas Chart

Idea	I like this idea.	I know about this idea	I want to learn more.

Use the chart to answer these questions.

Which ideas will you not choose? Why not?

Which ideas might you choose? Why?

Look at your answer for number 2.
Will you need to research those ideas before you can write?

Which writing idea do you choose?

Overview   Narrow the Writing Idea

Directions and Sample Answers for Activity Pages

Day 1	See "Provide a Real-World Example" below.
Day 2	Read the title and directions aloud. For students who struggle, suggest organizing the colors by color scheme such as reds, oranges, etc. Management Tip: Supply each pair of students with the same brand of 24-count crayons before the activity.
Day 3	Read the title and directions aloud. Invite students to look at the pictures. Then ask students to write a list of twelve things they think of when they see each picture. Remind students that there are no wrong answers. Students will use their ideas in the next lesson.
Day 4	Read the title and directions aloud. Invite students to review their lists from the previous lesson. Ask students to organize each list into groups and give each group a title. Finally, ask students to think about which group they would like to write about and circle that group.
Day 5	Read the directions aloud. Allow time for students to complete each task. Afterward, meet individually with students to discuss their results and to plan further instruction.

Provide a Real-World Example

◆ Hand out Day 1 activity page. **Say:** *I've decided to write about rocks. There are so many things about rocks that I like. How am I going to decide which idea to write about? Watch as I choose one thing to write about. First, I'll make a general list of things that have to do with rocks.* (Generate a list of "rock" ideas as shown.)

◆ **Say:** *Yikes. That's a long list. For me to make up my mind, I need to understand what I just wrote. I'm going to put these ideas into groups. I notice that I've identified the three main types of rocks and some examples of each. I'll write those in a list.*

◆ Repeat with other categories. Then review and label them as shown.

◆ **Say:** *Wow. I've just taken lost of ideas and organized them into categories. Now I need to decide what I'm going to write about. I don't really want to write about what rocks show or rock characteristics. I also don't think I want to write only about uses for rocks. Oh. I've got an idea. I think I'll write about the different types of rocks and include uses for each of those types. So I'll actually use two groups in my paper. Organizing my ideas really helped me make a good decision.*

Rocks

Metamorphic   Flint   Talc
Sedimentary   Volcanic   Used for buildings
Igneous   Black   Used for statues
Show weather   Smooth   Used for chalk
over time   Jagged   Used in powder
Show Earth's   Obsidian   Show's Earth's
movements   Basalt   history
over time   Marble
Limestone

Types of Rocks	What Rocks Show	Features of Rocks	Uses for Rocks
Igneous: obsidian, basalt	weather over time	Volcanic	Buildings
		Black	Statues
Metamorphic: marble, talc	Earth's movements over time	Smooth	Chalk
Sedimentary: limestone, flint	Earth's history	Jagged	Powder

Narrow the Writing Idea

Write a list of everything you think of when you hear the word "rocks."

Rocks

1. _____
2. _____
3. _____
4. _____
5. _____
6. _____
7. _____
8. _____
9. _____
10. _____
11. _____
12. _____
13. _____
14. _____
15. _____
16. _____
17. _____
18. _____
19. _____
20. _____

Group ideas into categories. Then give each group a title.

Title: _____	**Title:** _____	**Title:** _____	**Title:** _____
1. _____	1. _____	1. _____	1. _____
2. _____	2. _____	2. _____	2. _____
3. _____	3. _____	3. _____	3. _____
4. _____	4. _____	4. _____	4. _____
5. _____	5. _____	5. _____	5. _____

Organize Ideas

Read the list of colors from a box of 24 crayons. Organize the colors into groups.
You may use a real box of 24 crayons if you choose. Then give each group a title.

Yellow orange	Black
Green yellow	Blue
Yellow green	Dandelion
Red	Blue violet
Violet red	Brown
Purple	Green
Blue green	Red violet
Gray	Sky blue
Yellow	Orange
Red orange	Apricot
Indigo	Pink
Scarlet	White

Writing Your Ideas

Look at the pictures. For each picture, write twelve things that you think about when you see the picture.

1. _____	1. _____	1. _____
2. _____	2. _____	2. _____
3. _____	3. _____	3. _____
4. _____	4. _____	4. _____
5. _____	5. _____	5. _____
6. _____	6. _____	6. _____
7. _____	7. _____	7. _____
8. _____	8. _____	8. _____
9. _____	9. _____	9. _____
10. _____	10. _____	10. _____
11. _____	11. _____	11. _____
12. _____	12. _____	12. _____

Narrow the Focus

Organize your lists from Day 3 into groups. Give each group a label. Think about the groups and the specific ideas in each group. Which group would you like to write about? Why? Circle the group and share your thinking with a partner.

Assessment

Look at the picture. Under the picture, write twelve things that you think about when you see the picture.

1. _____   7. _____

2. _____   8. _____

3. _____   9. _____

4. _____   10. _____

5. _____   11. _____

6. _____   12. _____

In the space below, organize the list into groups. Then give each group a title. Think about each group. Which group would you like to write about most? Why?

Title: _____   **Title: _____**   **Title: _____**

_____   _____   _____

_____   _____   _____

_____   _____   _____

_____   _____   _____

_____   _____   _____

Overview Develop the Writing Idea

Directions and Sample Answers for Activity Pages

Day 1	See "Provide a Real-World Example" below.
Day 2	Read the title and directions aloud. Invite students to read the list of ideas. Ask them to identify four things that they already know about each idea. Ask students to write those ideas on the lines provided and share their ideas with a partner.
Day 3	Read the title and directions aloud. Invite students to look at the pictures. Tell students that each picture stands for a possible writing idea. Ask students to think about each idea and identify two questions for each idea that they would like answered. Have students write their questions on the lines provided. Remind students that each question could be used later to develop a writing idea.
Day 4	Read the title and directions aloud. Invite students to read the list of ideas. Ask students to research each idea using encyclopedias or the Internet and identify four things that they did not know about each idea. Have students write the information on the lines provided and share their thoughts with a partner.
Day 5	Read the directions aloud. Allow time for students to complete the task. Afterward, meet individually with students to discuss their results. Use their responses to plan further instruction.

Provide a Real-World Example

◆ Hand out the Day 1 activity page and write the word "types of rocks" on the board. **Say:** *I've decided to write about the three different types of rocks and their uses. I want to include certain things, so I need to plan, or develop, my idea before I write. Asking focus questions will help me plan.*

◆ Write focus question in a knowledge chart on the board as shown. **Say:** *I'll use a knowledge chart to help me plan my idea. Answers to these questions will help me plan my idea.*

◆ **Say:** *I know that there are three types of rocks. I also know that each of the three types of rocks has lots of different rocks. I know that rocks are used to make different things. I'll write those things into the chart. Is that all I want to include in my paper? No. That doesn't seem to be enough. So what questions do I have about rocks? I'll write those questions on the chart.* Circle the last column containing the questions.

◆ **Say:** *I don't have answers to questions in the last column. I'll need to do a little research on the Internet before I can write my paper. I can probably find information in the encyclopedia, but I like the Internet better so I'll use that.*

◆ Remind students that developing a writing idea takes time. Students should not hurry through this part of the writing process.

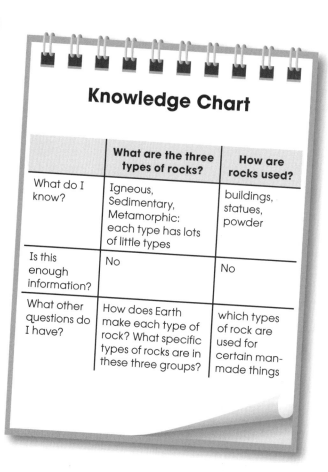

Knowledge Chart

	What are the three types of rocks?	How are rocks used?
What do I know?	Igneous, Sedimentary, Metamorphic: each type has lots of little types	buildings, statues, powder
Is this enough information?	No	No
What other questions do I have?	How does Earth make each type of rock? What specific types of rocks are in these three groups?	which types of rock are used for certain man-made things

Develop the Writing Idea

Complete the chart.

Knowledge Chart Focus Questions

	What are the three types of rocks?	How are rocks used?
What do I know?		
Is this enough information?		
What other questions do I have?		

What Do You Know About It?

Read the list of ideas. For each idea, identify four things that you already know. Write your ideas on the lines and share your information with a partner.

Native Americans

1. _____
2. _____
3. _____
4. _____

Animals of the sea

1. _____
2. _____
3. _____
4. _____

Movies

1. _____
2. _____
3. _____
4. _____

United States geography

1. _____
2. _____
3. _____
4. _____

Ask a Question... or Two

Look at the pictures. Each picture stands for a different writing idea. Think about two questions that you have for each idea. Write your questions on the lines and share them with a partner.

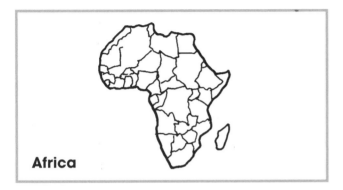

Africa

_____

_____

_____

camping

_____

_____

_____

desert

_____

_____

_____

cruise ship

_____

_____

_____

Research It

Read the list of ideas from Day 3. Use encyclopedias or the Internet to find out four things that you did not know about each idea. Write the information on the lines and share your ideas with a partner.

Africa

1. _____
2. _____
3. _____
4. _____

Camping

1. _____
2. _____
3. _____
4. _____

Desert

1. _____
2. _____
3. _____
4. _____

Cruise ship

1. _____
2. _____
3. _____
4. _____

Assessment

**Read the question. Fill in the blank with your favorite food.
Then complete the chart.**

Knowledge Chart

	What do I know about _____ ?	Is this enough information?	What questions do I have about _____ ?
What is my favorite food? My favorite food is _____ .			

Overview Develop an Outline of Information

Directions and Sample Answers for Activity Pages

Day 1	See "Provide a Real-World Example" below.
Day 2	Read the title and directions aloud. (Answers: foods for a healthy body; body organs; parts of the circulatory system; parts of the muscular system) Finally, ask students to choose one group of words and illustrate it. Then have students write a short paragraph explaining their illustration. Share drawings and paragraphs with a partner.
Day 3	Read the title and directions aloud. (Possible answers: hurricanes—fast winds, lots of rain, flooding; tornadoes—high winds, things flying in the air, destroyed buildings; blizzards—heavy snowfall, damaged buildings, power outages) Have students share their work.
Day 4	Read the title and directions aloud. (Possible answers: fresh water—rivers, lakes, streams; salt water—oceans, gulfs, bays; uses for water—drinking, cooking, power) Have students identify a favorite use for water, draw a picture of it, and explain their answer to a partner.
Day 5	Read the directions aloud. Allow time for students to complete each task. (Possible answers: where snakes live—desert, forest, water; what they eat—eggs, smaller animals; name three snakes—rattlesnake, copper mouth, boa constrictor) (Possible answers: how to handle a snake bite—cover with gauze, get to a hospital, don't move around a lot) Afterward, meet individually with students to discuss their results. Use their responses to plan further instruction.

Provide a Real-World Example

◆ Hand out the Day 1 activity page. **Ask:** *What does the word "organize" mean?* (Allow responses.)

◆ **Say:** *When authors write nonfiction, they organize information in a way that makes sense. First they write down big ideas. Then they write details that support the big ideas. We call this plan an outline. I want to write a short paper about the three rock types. Watch as I organize my information into a chart.* Use the chart below to show students how to organize information for rock types.

◆ **Say:** *The first thing I need to do is write down my big ideas. First, I think I need to define the three rock types and how they are formed. I might even include something interesting about each type. Next, I think I'll include different rocks that fall under the three rock types . . . maybe three. For this paper, I may even include drawings of those different rocks. Finally, I'll include information about how each type of rock is used today. Now I'll fill in each big idea.* Complete the chart.

◆ **Say:** *Wow! I wrote a lot. My next step is to write these ideas into complete sentences and work on my hook and ending. Remember to plan before you write. It makes writing easier.*

The Three Rock Types

Big Ideas	Details
define the three main types of rocks and how they are formed	Igneous: made with heat and fire. Sedimentary: made from sediment layers forming into rock over long periods of time Metamorphic: used to be igneous or sedimentary rock, but changed due to pressure inside Earth
examples of each type	Igneous: obsidian, pumice, granite Sedimentary: limestone, shale, sandstone Metamorphic: marble, gneiss, slate
which rocks are used to build or make things today	Igneous: pumice is used in hand soaps and nail files, granite is used for monuments and buildings Sedimentary: sandstone is a building material, limestone is used for cement and the base for roads Metamorphic: marble is used for countertops and as a building material, slate is used as a building material and for roof coverings

Develop an Outline of Information

1. Choose an idea—rocks

2. Narrow an idea—the three rock types

3. Develop an idea—what I know and don't know about the three rock types

4. Develop an outline—organize information to write

Complete the chart.

The Three Rock Types

Big Ideas	Details

What's the Big Idea?

Look at each group of words. Each group supports a big idea about the human body. Decide what the big idea is and write it on the lines. Share your big ideas with a partner. Explain how you got your answers.

vegetables

protein   Big Idea: _____

carbohydrates   _____

fruits

---

lungs

intestines   Big Idea: _____

stomach   _____

brain

---

blood

veins   Big Idea: _____

capillaries   _____

heart

---

ligaments

muscles   Big Idea: _____

tendons   _____

joints

Choose one group of words. Draw a picture that stands for the words in the group. Write a short paragraph explaining your picture. Share your paragraph and drawing with a partner.

Support the Big Idea

Look at the charts. Each chart tells something different about dangerous weather. There are three boxes under each big idea. For each box, write one detail that supports its big idea. Share your thinking with a partner.

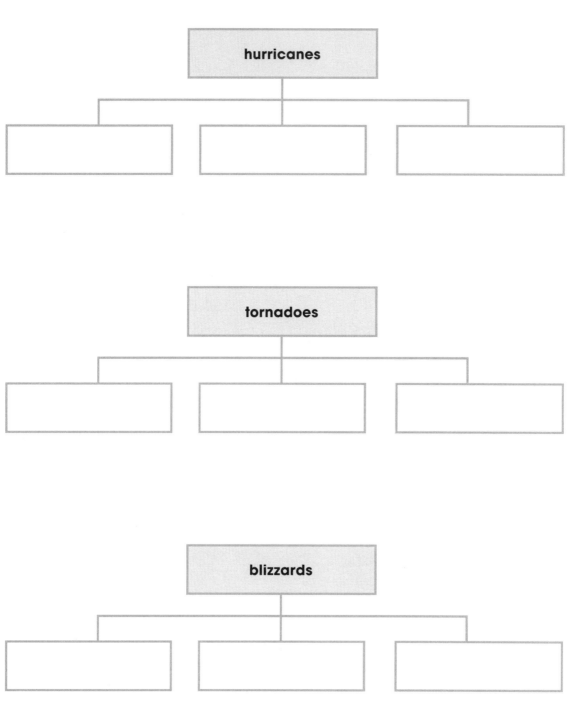

Choose one chart. Draw pictures that explain each detail.

Make an Outline

Look at the incomplete chart about water. Fill in the missing information.

Water

Big Ideas	Details
fresh water	
salt water	
uses for water	

What is your favorite use for water? Is it drinking, swimming, watering the yard? Draw a picture of it and explain your answer to your partner.

Assessment

Look at the incomplete chart about snakes. Fill in the missing information.

Snakes

Big Ideas	Details
where they live	
what they eat	
name three snakes	

Identify one more big idea for this chart and the details that support it.

Overview   Strong Nonfiction Leads

Directions and Sample Answers for Activity Pages

Day 1	See "Provide a Real-World Example" below.
Day 2	Read the title and directions aloud. Invite students to look at the chart and read the leads. Then ask students to analyze the leads and identify which lead they prefer. Finally, have students share their thinking with a partner.
Day 3	Read the title and directions aloud. Invite students to look at the pictures on the left side of the page. Then ask students to match each picture with its correct lead. Ask students to share their results with a partner. (Answers: hotdog—2; pigpen—4; stream—5; squid—3; forest in winter—1) Finally, ask students to choose one picture and write a different lead for it. Have students share their new lead with a partner. For an extra lesson, help students analyze the different types of leads used in this exercise. (1—describing a sound; 2—dialogue; 3—stating a fact; 4—using a question; 5—stating an opinion)
Day 4	Read the title and directions aloud. Invite students to look at the pictures. Then ask students to write a strong lead for each picture. If students struggle, have them review leads from Day 3 and offer assistance. Ask students to share their results with a partner. Finally, have students choose one picture and write a different lead for it. Then have students ask a partner to decide which picture matches the lead.
Day 5	Read the directions aloud. Allow time for students to complete the first task. Next, have students complete the second task. Afterward, meet individually with students to discuss their results. Use their responses to plan further instruction.

Provide a Real-World Example

◆ Hand out the Day 1 activity page. **Say:** *When authors write nonfiction, they begin with a sentence or two that makes readers want to keep reading. We call these sentences strong leads, or hooks.*

◆ **Say:** *Let's say that I'm going to write about a girl's best friend . . . diamonds. I've written two leads and can't decide which one to choose. Look at the leads on the board.*

◆ Have a student read the leads and help students analyze them and complete the chart using the information shown.

◆ **Ask:** *Which lead makes you want to read my paper? Why?* (Allow responses.)

◆ **Say:** *The second lead sounds more interesting than the first. I think my readers will want to read more about diamonds. Remember to use a strong leads to hook your reader.*

◆ Remind students that leads like "This paper is about . . ." or "I'm going to tell you about a . . ." are not strong leads.

Nonfiction Leads

Diamonds are pretty.	What sparkles in the light, is found in the ground, and is very expensive?
simply states what the author is writing about; doesn't offer any information about diamonds; weak lead	is written in question form; offers catchy information about diamonds; strong lead

Name _____

Strong Nonfiction Leads

Complete the chart.

Nonfiction Leads

Diamonds are pretty.	What sparkles in the light, is found in the ground, and is very expensive?

Name _____

Strong and Weak Nonfiction Leads

Read the nonfiction leads. Tell which lead is strong and which lead is weak. Explain your thinking on the chart. Answer the question at the bottom of the page and share your thinking with a partner.

Hamburgers

I'm going to tell you about hamburgers.	**Hamburgers. The word makes you think of juicy meat, melty cheese, ketchup, pickles, a bun, and, of course, french fries. Nothing tastes better.**

Which lead do you like better? Why?

_____

Lead Match-Up

Look at the pictures on the left side of the page. Each picture represents a nonfiction writing idea. Read the strong nonfiction leads on the right side of the page. Draw a line from the picture to its matching lead. Share your results with a partner.

Pictures	Strong Fiction Leads
	1. *Snap. Creak. Pop.* Snow can severely damage forested areas.
	2. "A hot dog!" the girl exclaimed. "Now that's lunch."
	3. This animal has a body like a large bullet, a goofy-looking head, and tentacles. Pretty strange.
	4. A pigpen next to a park? It's obvious that one of them has to go. Let me tell you the facts.
	5. Streams are beautiful places, but what's more beautiful is the tasty trout you can catch.

Choose one picture and write a different lead for it.

Share your lead with a partner.

Write-a-Lead

Look at the pictures. Each picture stands for a nonfiction writing idea. Write a strong nonfiction lead for each picture and share your leads with a partner.

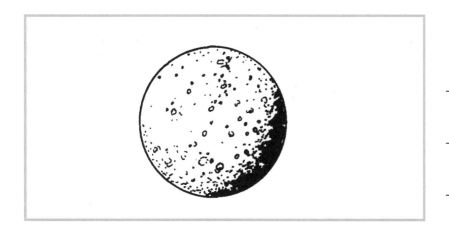

_____

_____

_____

_____

_____

_____

_____

_____

_____

Choose one picture and write a different lead for it. Share your lead with a partner and let him or her decide which picture matches the lead.

Assessment

Read the nonfiction leads. Tell which lead is strong and which lead is weak.
Explain what makes each lead strong or weak.

Stars

Stars twinkle in the night sky.	Glimmer. Glisten. Glow. That's what stars look like in the night sky.

Look at the picture and write a strong nonfiction lead.

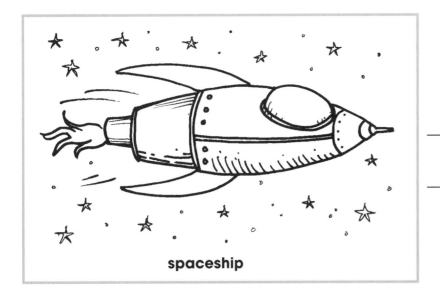

spaceship

_____

_____

Overview Strong Nonfiction Endings

Directions and Sample Answers for Activity Pages

Day 1	See "Provide a Real-World Example" below.
Day 2	Read the title and directions aloud. Invite students to look at the chart and read the endings. Then ask students to analyze the endings and identify which ending they prefer. Finally, have students share their thinking with a partner.
Day 3	Read the title and directions aloud. (Answers: bad dream—2; White House—1; beach with trash—4; skier—5; fingerprint—3) Finally, ask students to choose one picture and write a different ending for it. Have students share their new ending with a partner. For an extra lesson, help students analyze the different types of endings used in this exercise. (1 and 2—restate an important idea, 3—summarize information, 4—call to action, 5—make an observation)
Day 4	Read the title and directions aloud. If students struggle, have them review endings from Day 3 and offer assistance. Ask students to share their results with a partner. Finally, have students choose one picture and write a different ending for it. Then have students ask a partner to decide which picture matches the ending.
Day 5	Read the directions aloud. Allow time for students to complete each task. Afterward, meet individually with students to discuss their results. Use their responses to plan further instruction.

Provide a Real-World Example

◆ Hand out the Day 1 activity page. **Say:** *When authors write nonfiction, they begin with a sentence or two that makes readers want to keep reading. We call these sentences strong leads, or hooks. Writers also want to end with sentences that keep their readers thinking. Let's say that I've written a paper about hurricanes. I've written two endings and can't decide which one to choose. Look at the endings on the board.*

◆ Have one student read the endings and help students analyze them and complete the chart using the following information.

◆ **Ask:** *Which ending makes you think about how dangerous hurricanes can be? Why?* (Allow responses.) **Say:** *The second ending sounds more interesting than the first. I think my readers will think about hurricanes after reading my paper because I described them and added a piece of advice. They might think back to a hurricane they have lived through or one that they have read or heard about. Remember to use a strong ending to help your readers think.*

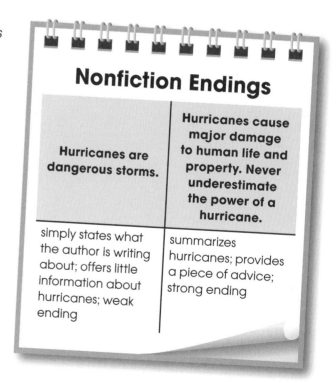

Nonfiction Endings

Hurricanes are dangerous storms.	Hurricanes cause major damage to human life and property. Never underestimate the power of a hurricane.
simply states what the author is writing about; offers little information about hurricanes; weak ending	summarizes hurricanes; provides a piece of advice; strong ending

Strong Nonfiction Endings

Complete the chart.

Nonfiction Endings

Hurricanes are dangerous storms.	Hurricanes cause major damage to human life and property. Never underestimate the power of a hurricane.

Strong and Weak Nonfiction Endings

Read the nonfiction endings. Tell which ending is strong and which ending is weak. Explain your thinking. Answer the question at the bottom of the page and share your thinking with a partner.

Chimpanzees

Chimpanzees are like us.	Chimpanzees live in communities, have feelings, and have jobs. That sounds a lot like humans.

Which ending do you like better? Why?

_____

Ending Match-Up

Look at the pictures on the left side of the page. Each picture stands for a nonfiction writing idea. Read the nonfiction endings on the right side of the page. Draw a line from the picture to its matching ending. Share your results with a partner.

bad dream

White House

1. Men from all walks of life have sat in the Oval Office of the White House. Now that's American.

2. Yes. Our emotions are a part of us, but we do not have to let them control us.

3. Fingerprints may have three main forms, but they are as different as the human race.

4. We do not have to put up with trash on our beaches. Let's find a way to end this.

5. Bravery. That's what it takes to ski down a mountain.

Choose one picture and write a different ending for it. Share you ending with a partner.

Write-an-Ending

Look at the pictures. Each picture stands for a nonfiction writing idea. Write a strong nonfiction ending for each picture and share your endings with a partner.

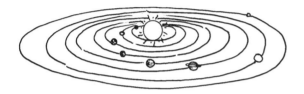

_____

_____

_____

_____

_____

_____

Choose one picture and write a different ending for it. Share your ending with a partner and let him or her decide which picture matches the ending.

Name _____

Assessment

Read the nonfiction endings. Tell which ending is strong and which ending is weak. Explain what makes each ending strong or weak.

Railroads

Everything about railroads is interesting.	Railroads carry people, produce, and products thousands of miles. They truly transformed America.

Look at the picture and write a strong nonfiction ending.

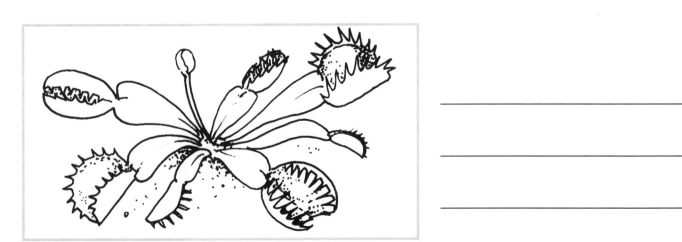

_____

_____

_____

 Unit 6 • Everyday Writing Intervention Activities Grade 5 • ©2011 Newmark Learning, LLC

Overview   Develop a Plot

Directions and Sample Answers for Activity Pages

Day 1	See "Provide a Real-World Example" below.
Day 2	Read the title and directions aloud. Invite students to thinks about a story idea that they might like to write about. Remind students to ask themselves questions such as where does the story take place and what does the setting look like. Then ask students to draw the setting. Finally, have students share their drawings with a partner.
Day 3	Read the title and directions aloud. Invite students to read the short stories. Then ask students to complete the stories by drawing the missing events. Finally, have students share their drawings with a partner.
Day 4	Read the title and directions aloud. Invite students to read the story events. Have students order the events from 1 to 11. Have students share their thinking with a partner. (Answer: 5, 2, 8, 4, 11, 9, 1, 10, 6, 7, 3)
Day 5	Read the directions aloud. Allow time for students to complete each task. Afterward, meet individually with students to discuss their results and to plan further instruction.

Provide a Real-World Example

◆ Hand out the Day 1 activity page. **Say:** *What makes a story interesting to you?* (Allow responses.)

◆ **Say:** *The things, or events, that happen in a story are called the plot. Good authors spend time planning, or developing, a plot before they start writing.*

◆ Use the information in the chart to show students how to develop the time, place, and introduction to a short story. **Say:** *The first thing I need to do is decide on my setting which is time and place. Then I'll develop the plot for the rest of the story.*

◆ Explain that each event connects to the next event and the problem pushes the story. Point out the problem and the resolution. Then **say:** *The last thing I need to do is decide how my story will end. This is called the conclusion. Not only do the kids get to go to a carnival, but they spent a whole morning on an adventure. Let me write in my conclusion.*

◆ **Say:** *Remember that this chart just shows my big events and ideas. To write a really good short story, I need to include details about the setting, characters, and events. All of these things will keep my readers interested.*

Plot Chart

Time	present time during summer vacation (morning)
Place	island with a great beach and a wooded area nearby with a small cave
Introduction	a brother and sister are playing at the beach, bored, they discover an old green bottle
Story Events (Plot)	They open the bottle and find a note inside that tells them to go to the cave.
	They decide an adventure would be fun, so they go to the cave.
	At the cave the kids find a pile of old fish bones and a note that tells them to enter the cave and go forward fifty paces—they're a little nervous, but decide to go.
	Fifty paces inside the cave, they find a note and a shovel, the note tells them to dig a hole that is three feet deep and two feet wide.
	The kids take turns digging and find a box—they open the box and find two tickets to the carnival in town.
Conclusion	They run home and show their mom and dad. That's when they find out that the parents planned the whole adventure.

Develop a Plot

Complete the plot chart.

Plot Chart

Time	
Place	
Introduction	
Story Events (Plot)	
Conclusion	

Unit 7 • Everyday Writing Intervention Activities Grade 5 • ©2011 Newmark Learning, LLC

Draw a Setting

Think of a story idea that you might like to write about. Where does your story take place? What does the setting look like? In the space below, use crayons, pencils, and/or markers to draw your setting. Remember, the more details you include the better your drawing, and writing, will be.

What happened?

Read the stories. For each story, two events are missing. Draw the missing events in the boxes. Share your drawings with a partner.

Story #1

1st event   Juan didn't know if he should be standing at the base of the volcano. It had rumbled all night long. What if it erupted? Juan looked over to his left. What he saw scared him half to death. He turned and ran back to the village. He had to warn everyone.

2nd event	3rd event

4th event   By the next day, the village was covered in volcanic ash, but everyone, including brave Juan, was safe.

Story #2

1st event   "I don't know," Alan said sadly. "Maybe I shouldn't go to the fair with Jim. The baseball team really needs me to practice. I wouldn't want to be the reason we lose the big game."

2nd event	3rd event

4th event   "I'm glad I decided to go to practice," Alan thought to himself. "It was the right thing to do."

Plot Order

The story below is about two kids and their adventure in a spooky, old house. Read the story events. They are out of order. Order the events from 1 to 11.

_____   They ran into the house and the front door slammed shut behind them.

_____   When they reached the front door, Mary whispered, "It's now or never."

_____   Just then, a huge pumpkin tumbled down the stairs and landed right at their feet.

_____   "Put your jacket over your head and run inside," Jack yelled to Mary. "I'll follow you."

_____   "What did you see?" Sam asked eagerly. "You don't want to know," replied Mary.

_____   The kids took off running down the hill . . . screaming the whole way.

_____   Mary and Jack knew they shouldn't go up there, but they couldn't resist a challenge.

_____   When they got to the bottom of the hill, Sam and Lane were waiting for them.

_____   They found themselves in a huge room filled with cobwebs and dust.

_____   "Remember, all we have to do is run around the first floor of the house," Mary said.

_____   Jack opened the door, and bats flew at them.

Assessment

Read the plot chart. Some information is missing. Complete the chart.

Plot Chart

Time	3:00 in the afternoon
Place	the school bus coming home from school
Introduction	Michael is on his way home from school; he hears the burglar alarm to his house
Story Events (Plot)	Michael jumps off the bus and runs to the neighbor's house
Conclusion	

Read the story events. Two events are missing. Draw the missing events in the boxes provided.

1st event

James is finishing his homework at the kitchen table when his dog, Casper, runs up to him and barks loudly.

2nd event

3rd event

4th event

Casper proudly stands at the back door with a dead baby rattlesnake hanging from his mouth.

Overview   Develop a Character

Directions and Sample Answers for Activity Pages

Day 1	See "Provide a Real-World Example" below.
Day 2	Read the title and directions aloud. Have students share their work with a partner.
Day 3	Read the title and directions aloud. Invite students to look at the two sets of character pictures. Ask students what they think might have happened to change the character. Then ask them to write their ideas on the lines between the two pictures. Finally, have students share their thinking with a partner.
Day 4	Read the title and directions aloud. To the side of each web, ask students to draw pictures of how the character changes. Remind students to think about how she changes over time. Have students share their drawings with a partner.
Day 5	Read the directions aloud. Allow time for students to complete each task. Afterward, meet individually with students to discuss their results and to plan further instruction.

Provide a Real-World Example

◆ Hand out the Day 1 activity page. **Say:** *Good writers make a plan for each character before they start writing. They decide what the characters will look like and how they will act. These are called character traits. Then as the story develops, so do the characters. They may keep the same traits or change traits because of story events.*

◆ **Say:** *This is a character chart on Adam. He's in a story I want to write. Adam is a funny guy. He makes people laugh and doesn't take life seriously. Adam also likes to pull practical jokes. Sometimes, his practical jokes can be mean. When I write my story, I'll be sure to include all of these things and include details that support my character traits.* Complete the first "Adam" character web.

◆ **Say:** *I want my story to be interesting, so I need something to happen . . . I need a problem. Maybe my problem is that Adam pulls a practical joke on a friend. The friend gets hurt and tells the teacher.* Help students revise Adam's character web to match the problem.

◆ **Say:** *I need to keep my story moving, so I need to resolve the problem. Well, I'm guessing Adam has some sort of punishment. In my story, Adam realizes that practical jokes are not always funny and people can get hurt or get in trouble . . . or both. He apologizes to his friend and his teacher. Now, Adam thinks about how his actions can hurt others.* Help students revise Adam's character web to match the resolution.

◆ **Say:** *A character's actions match what is happening in the story. For a character to develop, the author keeps both character and story events in mind when writing.*

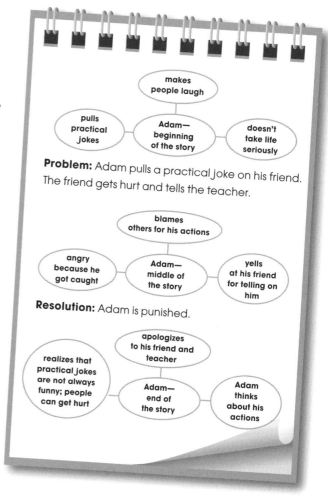

Problem: Adam pulls a practical joke on his friend. The friend gets hurt and tells the teacher.

Resolution: Adam is punished.

Develop a Character

Complete the character webs.

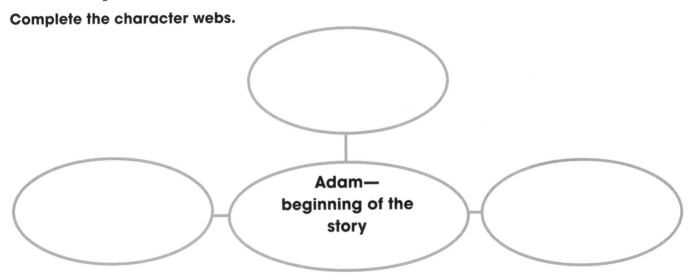

Problem: Adam pulls a practical joke on his friend. The friend gets hurt and tells the teacher.

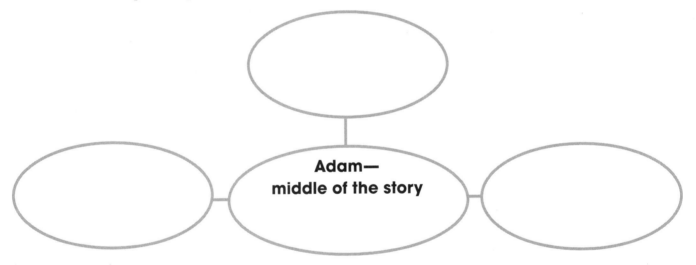

Resolution: Adam is punished.

Characters Change . . . But Why?

Look at the pictures and read the sentences. Draw how you think the problem might affect the character. Share your drawings with a partner.

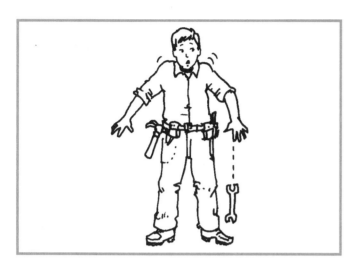

Problem: The man drops a wrench on his foot. How is the man affected by his actions?

Problem: A boy pulls a girl's pigtails. How is the boy affected by his actions?

Problem: A boy brings flowers to his grandmother who is in the hospital. How is the boy affected by his actions?

What Happened?

Look at the two sets of character pictures. What do you think might have
happened to change the character? Write your ideas in between the pictures.
Share your thoughts with a partner.

_____
_____
_____

_____
_____
_____

_____
_____
_____

Develop a Character

Look at the character webs. They tell how a character named Maria changes in a story. Think about how each web describes Maria. For each web, draw pictures that show what you think Maria looks like. Share your illustrations with a partner.

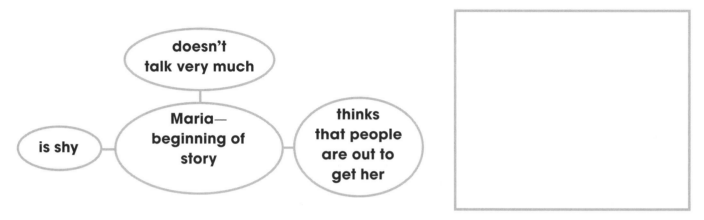

Problem: The school librarian tells Maria that she has an overdue book. Maria knows she's turned it in, but can't prove it.

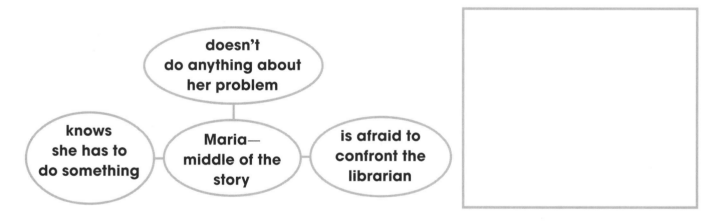

Resolution: Maria's neighbor tells her that she must be strong and talk to the librarian. She must stand up for what she believes. Maybe the book is already on the shelf.

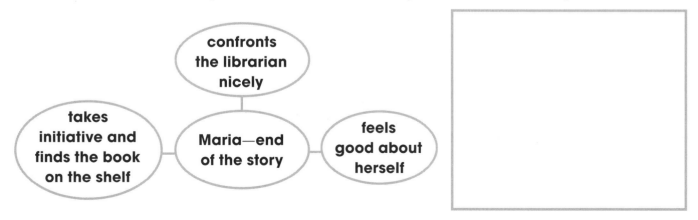

Assessment

Read the first character web. Use it to develop the same character in the other character webs.

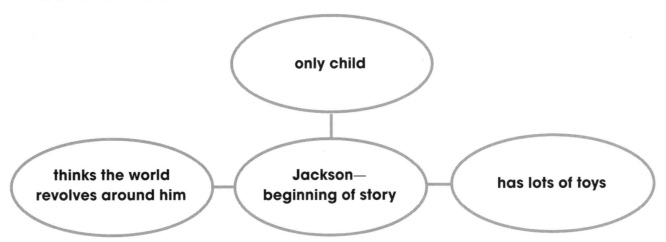

Problem: Jackson's mom has a baby boy. They name the baby Jordan.

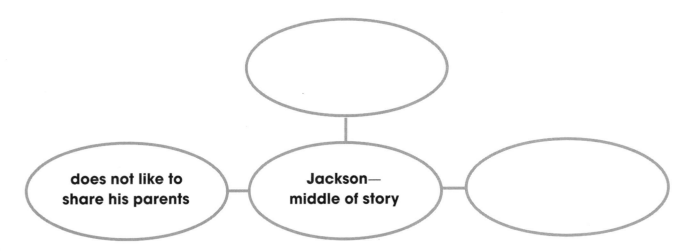

Resolution: After several weeks, Jordan smiles at Jackson.

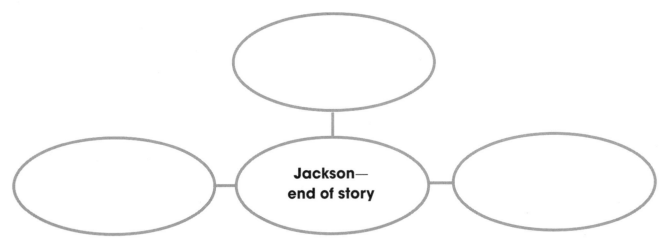

Unit 8 • Everyday Writing Intervention Activities Grade 5 • ©2011 Newmark Learning, LLC

Overview Strong Fiction Leads

Directions and Sample Answers for Activity Pages

Day 1	See "Provide a Real-World Example" below.
Day 2	Read the title and directions aloud. Invite students to look at the chart and read the leads. Then ask students to analyze the leads and identify which lead they prefer. Finally, have students share their thinking with a partner.
Day 3	Read the title and directions aloud. Invite students to look at the pictures on the left side of the page. Then ask students to match each picture with its correct lead. Ask students to share their results with a partner. (Answers: kids with TV—3; football players—5; baby with phone—4; unmade bed—1; four kids in a car—2) Finally, ask students to choose one picture and write a different lead for it. Have students share their new lead with a partner. For an extra lesson, help students analyze the different types of leads used in this exercise. (1—question, 2—opinion, 3—dialogue, 4—describing a sound, 5—telling a fact)
Day 4	Read the title and directions aloud. Invite students to look at the pictures. Then ask students to write a strong lead for each picture. If students struggle, have them review leads from Day 3 and offer assistance. Ask students to share their results with a partner. Finally, have students choose one picture and write a different lead for it. Then have students ask a partner to decide which picture matches the lead.
Day 5	Read the directions aloud. Allow time for students to complete each task. Afterward, meet individually with students to discuss their results. Use their responses to plan further instruction.

Provide a Real-World Example

◆ Hand out the Day 1 activity page. **Say:** *When authors write stories, they begin with a sentence or two that makes readers want to keep reading. We call these sentences strong leads, or hooks.*

◆ **Say:** *Let's say that I'm going to write a story about a boy and his fish. I've written two leads and can't decide which one to choose. Look at the leads on the board.*

◆ Have a student read the leads and help students analyze them by completing the chart. Use the information here.

◆ **Ask:** *Which lead makes you want to read my story? Why?* (Allow responses.)

◆ **Say:** *The second lead sounds more interesting than the first. I think my readers will want to find out what happened to the boy and his fish. Remember to use a strong lead that hooks readers.*

◆ Remind students that leads like "This story is about . . . " or "I'm going to tell you a story about a . . ." are not strong leads.

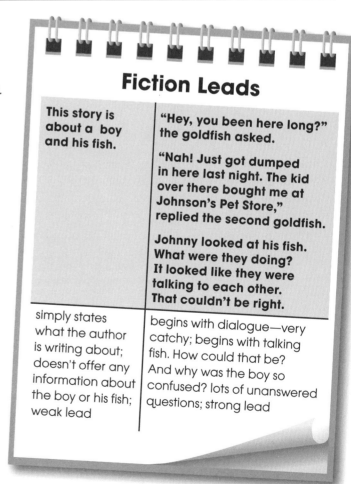

Fiction Leads

This story is about a boy and his fish.	"Hey, you been here long?" the goldfish asked. "Nah! Just got dumped in here last night. The kid over there bought me at Johnson's Pet Store," replied the second goldfish. Johnny looked at his fish. What were they doing? It looked like they were talking to each other. That couldn't be right.
simply states what the author is writing about; doesn't offer any information about the boy or his fish; weak lead	begins with dialogue—very catchy; begins with talking fish. How could that be? And why was the boy so confused? lots of unanswered questions; strong lead

Name _____

Strong Fiction Leads

Complete the chart.

Fiction Leads

This story is about a boy and his fish.	"Hey, you been here long?" the goldfish asked. "Nah! Just got dumped in here last night. The kid over there bought me at Johnson's Pet Store," replied the second goldfish. Johnny looked at his fish. What were they doing? It looked like they were talking to each other. That couldn't be right.

Strong and Weak Fiction Leads

Read the story leads. Tell which lead is strong and which lead is weak. Explain your thinking in the space provided. Answer the question at the bottom of the page and share your thinking with a partner.

Sleepless

I was awake all night.	*Drip. Drip. Drip.* Would that faucet quit making that sound? I was going to be awake all night.

Which lead do you like better? Why?

_____

Fiction Lead Match-Up

Look at the pictures on the left side of the page. Each picture represents a story. Read the strong fiction leads on the right side of the page. Draw a line from the picture to its matching lead. Share your thinking with a partner.

1. Didn't I just tell you to make that bed?

2. Four kids in a car is not a good thing.

3. "What a boring day!" I complained. "Are we going to do anything other than watch TV?"

4. *Brrring Brrring. Brring.* The baby looked at the phone as she made that cute sound.

5. Both teams were playing well. But one thing was for sure . . . both teams could not win the game.

Choose one picture and write a different lead for it. Share your lead with a partner.

Write-a-Lead

Look at the pictures. Each picture stands for a story. Write a strong story lead for each picture and share your leads with a partner.

_____

_____

_____

_____

_____

_____

Choose one picture and write a different lead for it. Share your lead with a partner and let him or her decide which picture matches the lead.

Assessment

Read the following story leads. Tell which lead is strong and which lead is weak. Explain what makes each lead strong or weak.

The Worst Day Ever

This story is about the worst day ever.	It looked like the day would turn out to be perfect.

Look at the picture from a story. Write a strong lead for the story.

_____

_____

_____

_____

_____

Overview   Strong Fiction Endings

Directions and Sample Answers for Activity Pages

Day 1	See "Provide a Real-World Example" below.
Day 2	Read the title and directions aloud. Invite students to look at the chart and read the endings. Then ask students to analyze the endings and identify which ending they prefer. Finally, have students share their thinking with a partner.
Day 3	Read the title and directions aloud. Invite students to look at the pictures on the left side of the page. Then ask students to match each picture with its correct ending. Ask students to share their results with a partner. (Answers: cafeteria—5; hand bell choir—3; erupting volcano—4; little girl and neighbor—1; ant farm—2) Finally, ask students to choose one picture and write a different lead for it. Have students share their new lead with a partner. For an extra lesson, help students analyze the different types of leads used in this exercise. (Answers: 1—restating an important idea in the story; 2—life goes on; 3—personal observation; 4—waiting nervously; 5—humor)
Day 4	Read the title and directions aloud. Invite students to look at the pictures. Then ask students to write a strong ending for each picture. If students struggle, have them review endings from Day 3 and offer assistance. Ask students to share their results with a partner. Finally, have students choose one picture and write a different lead for it. Then have students ask a partner to decide which picture matches the lead.
Day 5	Read the directions aloud. Allow time for students to complete each task. Afterward, meet individually with students to discuss their results. Use their responses to plan further instruction.

Provide a Real-World Example

◆ Hand out the Day 1 activity page. **Say:** *When authors write stories, they begin with a sentence or two that make readers want to keep reading. We call these sentences strong leads, or hooks. Writers also want to end with sentences that keep their readers thinking. Let's say that I have written a story about a girl who was in the hospital. Visitors have stopped by and one visitor even brought flowers. Unfortunately, a bee liked the flowers a lot and stung the girl. I've written two endings and can't decide which one to choose. Look at the endings on the board.*

◆ Have one student read the endings and help students analyze them and complete the chart using the following information.

◆ **Ask:** *Which ending makes you think? Why?* (Allow responses.)

◆ **Say:** *The second ending sounds more interesting than the first. The second ending reminds me of what happened to the girl. It also helps me remember that tomorrow is always another day. Just because bad things happen on one day does not mean that good things can't happen the next day.*

◆ Remind students that endings like "My story is done" or "This is the end of my story" are not strong endings.

Fiction Endings

I was glad to get out of the hospital.	I don't think I will ever look at flowers the same way again.
simply states that the author has finished writing the story; doesn't leave the reader thinking; weak ending	makes a humorous statement; might make readers remember when they've received flowers or been stung by a bee; strong ending

Name _____

Strong Fiction Endings

Complete the chart.

Fiction Endings

I was glad to get out of the hospital.	I don't think I will ever look at flowers the same way again.

Strong and Weak Fiction Endings

These endings complete a story about a cat who likes to take baths.
Read the endings. Tell which ending is strong and which ending is weak.
Explain your thinking on the chart. Answer the question at the bottom of the
page and share your thinking with a partner.

The Cat Bath

I want another bath tomorrow.	I might have gotten hair all over the bathtub. I might have gotten water all over my fur. But, oh, how wonderful it was to take a bath.

Which ending do you like better? Why?

_____

Story Ending Match-Up

**Look at the pictures on the left side of the page. Each picture represents a story.
Read the strong endings on the right side of the page. Draw a line from the
picture to its matching ending. Share your results with a partner.**

1. It's true. It takes a village to raise a child.

2. Well, what are you going to do? Ants get out when you don't put the lid on the ant farm.

3. "Practice makes perfect," Ann thought to herself. "And it's great to practice with friends."

4. The eruption lasted for days. Finally, we were able to return to our homes. But what would we find?

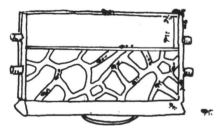

5. "Ahhhh. They've finally gone home," the chair said. "Yes! But they'll be back tomorrow," replied the table. "No they won't. Tomorrow is Saturday," the chair said with a sigh of relief.

Choose one picture and write a different ending for it. Share you ending with a partner.

Write-an-Ending

Look at the pictures. Each picture stands for a story. Write a strong ending for each picture and share them with a partner.

_____

_____

_____

_____

_____

_____

_____

_____

_____

_____

_____

_____

Choose one picture and write a different ending for it. Share your ending with a partner and let him or her decide which picture matches the ending.

Assessment

Read the story endings. Tell which ending is strong and which ending is weak. Explain what makes each ending strong or weak.

Cleaning House

I did not like cleaning house.	Cleaning house wasn't all that fun, but it was great fun cleaning with my cousins.

Look at the picture from a story. Write a strong ending for the story.

_____

_____

_____

Overview Using Voice

Directions and Sample Answers for Activity Pages

Day 1	See "Provide a Real-World Example" below.
Day 2	Read the title and directions aloud. Invite students to read the scene. Then ask students to choose a partner and act out what the objects might say to each other. Remind students to use voice. Finally, have each student choose one scene and write the conversation on the lines. (Partners do not need to choose the same scene.)
Day 3	Read the title and directions aloud. Invite students to choose a partner and read each sentence. Ask pairs to decide how the sentences might be said to their teacher and to their friend. Then have partners act out the sentence—once to their teacher and then to friends. Finally, have students choose one sentence and write it down the way they said it to their teacher and to their friend. (Partners do not need to choose the same sentence.)
Day 4	Read the title and directions aloud. Invite students to read the sentence pairs. Ask students to think about who the audience for each sentence might be. Have students write the audience on the line and share their results with a partner. Finally, have students choose one sentence and illustrate it.
Day 5	Read the directions aloud. Allow time for students to complete the task. Afterward, meet individually with students. Ask students to share responses with you. Discuss their results. Use their responses to plan further instruction.

Provide a Real-World Example

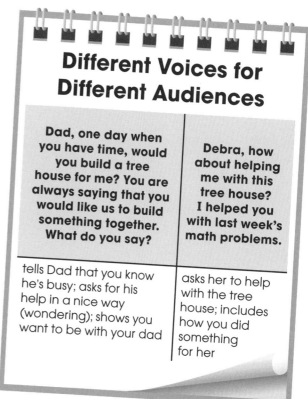

Different Voices for Different Audiences

Dad, one day when you have time, would you build a tree house for me? You are always saying that you would like us to build something together. What do you say?	Debra, how about helping me with this tree house? I helped you with last week's math problems.
tells Dad that you know he's busy; asks for his help in a nice way (wondering); shows you want to be with your dad	asks her to help with the tree house; includes how you did something for her

- ◆ Hand out the Day 1 activity page. **Ask:** *When we write, we want our words to sound like the way we would really speak. This is called voice. Think about how you would ask your dad to build a tree house for you. Would you use a gentle voice? A mean voice? What words might you use?*

- ◆ **Say:** *Now let's think about voice in a different way. Let's pretend that I'm asking my best friend to help me build the tree house. I see her every day. We talk all the time. The way I speak to my best friend is nice, but I don't speak to her the same way that I speak to my dad. My best friend is a different audience.*

- ◆ **Say:** *The note to my dad and the note to Debra say the same thing, but they sound very different. Let's analyze them.*

- ◆ **Say:** *These notes are written for different kinds of people so they should sound different. This is an example of using different voices for different audiences. What is an audience?* (Allow responses.)

- ◆ **Say:** *Yes. That's right. An audience is someone who is watching you perform. An audience might watch you perform in a dance recital, a karate match, a soccer game, or a play. An audience is also the person who reads what you write. Writing audiences can be a friend, a principal, a parent or grandparent, a teacher, or even the president of the United States. Remember your audience when you write so that you will use the right voice.*

Using Voice

Complete the chart.

Different Voices for Different Audiences

Dad, one day when you have time, would you build a tree house for me? You are always saying that you would like us to build something together. What do you say?	Debra, how about helping me with this tree house? I helped you with last week's math problems.

Using Voice

Read the scenes. With your partner, act out a short conversation that might happen between the two objects. Remember that each object has a voice.

1. pizza and a mouth

2. raisin and walnut cookie (conversation between the raisins and walnuts)

3. dirty bathtub and bathroom cleaner

4. a baseball and a bat

Choose one scene and write the conversation on the lines.

_____

_____

_____

_____

_____

_____

Voice Choice

**Read the sentence. Who might say this sentence? A father? A brother? A friend?
Each person would say that sentence in a different voice and use different words.**

> The car is almost out of gas.

A father might sternly say,
"Johnny, the car is almost out of gas. Be sure to fill it up."

A brother might whisper and say,
"Johnny, Dad told you to fill up the car with gas."

A friend might yell from the backseat,
"Hey, Johnny. The gas gauge is on E. Time to fill 'er up.

**Read each sentence. Decide how you would rephrase the sentence and
say it to your teacher and to your friend. Then act out the sentences with
your partner.**

1. I got a C? How did that happen?
2. The ball bounced on the school's roof.
3. There's a mouse in the corner of the classroom.
4. I forgot my homework.

**Choose one sentence. Write how you said the sentence to your teacher.
Then write how you said the sentence to your friend.**

_____

_____

_____

_____

How Would You Say It?

Read the sentence pairs. Decide who the audience might be.
Write your answer on the line. Share your answers with a partner.

Example:

This steak is great. How did you make it? (chef)

This steak is wonderful. I wonder how it was made. (friend)

1. May I borrow a pencil, please? _____

   Hey, you got a pencil I can borrow? _____

2. Oh no! I dropped a jar of pickles. _____

   I'm so sorry, but I dropped a jar of pickles in aisle ten. _____

3. Modeling clay comes up easily. _____

   Why is modeling clay all over the kitchen table? _____

4. I made my bed. _____

   Get in here and make your bed before your mom sees it. _____

Choose one sentence. Draw a picture of the sentence that includes
the audience. Share your picture with a friend.

Assessment

Write a sentence that matches the scene. Remember to use the right voice for the audience.

1. Tell your mom you finished sweeping the kitchen floor.

   _____

   Tell your friend you finished sweeping the kitchen floor.

   _____

2. Tell your teacher that the class needs more tissues.

   _____

   Tell your mom that the class needs more tissues.

   _____

3. Tell your cat that you are getting treats for her.

   _____

   Tell your little sister that you've made her a treat.

   _____

4. Ask your mom if you can play next door.

   _____

   Ask the neighbors if you can play next door.

   _____

Overview Adjectives

Directions and Sample Answers for Activity Pages

Day 1	See "Provide a Real-World Example" below.
Day 2	Read the title and directions aloud. Have students share illustrations with a partner. For extra credit, ask students to write a descriptive sentence and have a partner illustrate it.
Day 3	Read the title and directions aloud. Remind students that they want to write sentences that help their readers feel or see something. Have students share revised sentences with a partner.
Day 4	Read the title and directions aloud. Have students share their adjectives with a partner. Remind students that they want to write sentences that help their readers feel or see something.
Day 5	Read the directions aloud. Allow time for students to complete the first task. (Possible answer choices: 1. beautiful; ugly, 2. young; new, 3. wood; antique, 4. messy; stinky). Next, have students complete the second task. (Possible answers: The little boy's room was clean with everything in its place. I don't think Jennie liked that sour-tasting lemonade.) Afterward, meet individually with students. Ask students to share responses with you. Discuss their results. Use their responses to plan further instruction.

Provide a Real-World Example

◆ Hand out the Day 1 activity page. **Say:** *Authors use words to describe their ideas. They want readers to understand and feel something about what they write. They want readers to see what they see. Choosing specific adjectives that clearly describe the way something looks or the way it makes you feel is one way to accomplish this goal.*

◆ **Say:** *Look at the sentences. Does this sentence help us feel anything about the bell? Does it help us see the bell? No. It simply states where the bell is located, that it doesn't ring, and that it has hung there for a long time. These sentences don't describe anything. But, by adding a few adjectives and changing a few words, I can make the sentences more interesting and help my readers feel something about the bell and see the bell.*

◆ Write the following revised sentences on the board:

The famous Liberty Bell hangs on display in Philadelphia, Pennsylvania. Though silent, the copper-looking bell rings out "freedom" to all Americans.

Adjectives

Adjectives Describe . . .	Examples
how someone or something looks, feels, smells, tastes, or sounds	dirty, prickly, stinky, bitter, raspy, proud, worried, massive, curved, copper-looking, silent, old
what kind	famous, alive, dead, clever, sneaky
how many	several, few, ten

◆ **Say:** *How did I change the sentences? What adjectives did I use? How did they help the description? Remember, authors want readers to feel something about what they write. They want readers to see what they see. Choosing specific adjectives helps them accomplish this goal.*

◆ Help students generate examples of different types of adjectives and complete the chart.

Adjectives

Rewrite the sentences to include adjectives.

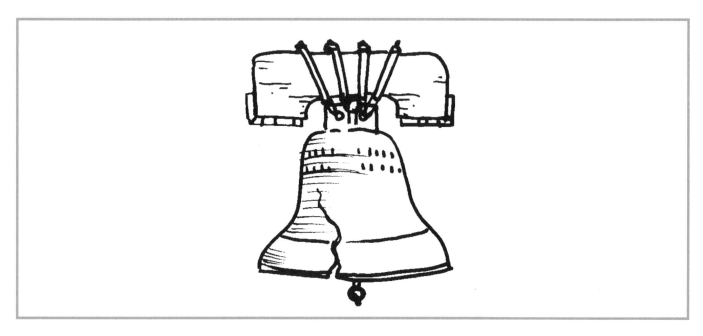

The Liberty Bell hangs on display in Philadelphia, Pennsylvania. It does not work. It has been there a long time.

_____

_____

_____

Adjectives Describe . . .	Examples
how someone or something looks, feels, smells, tastes, or sounds	
what kind	
how many	

Unit 12 • *Everyday Writing Intervention Activities Grade 5* • ©2011 Newmark Learning, LLC

Picture This

Read the sentences. Then draw a picture for each sentence.

1. Flaky snow blew through the oak tree's leafless branches.

2. An excited child ran up and down the long grocery store aisles.

3. In the pasture, a black and white Holstein cow lay in the carpet-like grass.

4. Please don't bring that wild cat into the house.

Write a descriptive sentence below. Share your sentence with a partner. Next to the sentence, have your partner draw a picture that illustrates the sentence.

_____

_____

_____

Using Adjectives

Read the sentences. Revise the sentences by including two adjectives.
Share your revised sentences with a partner.

1. The butterfly flew from our house to a tree.

_____

_____

2. A ball rolled in front of our car.

_____

_____

3. Our dog tripped the cat.

_____

_____

4. The flag blew in the wind.

_____

_____

Describing Objects

Look at the illustrations. Talk about them with a partner. Then choose two adjectives that describe each illustration and write it on the line provided. Share your adjectives with your partner.

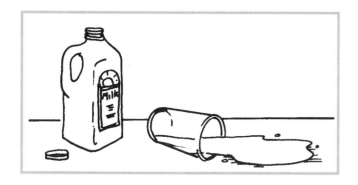

_____

_____

_____

_____

_____

_____

_____

_____

Choose two illustrations and write sentences about each one using your adjective choices. Share your sentences with your partner.

_____

_____

Assessment

Read the sentences. Make changes by adding two adjectives to each sentence.

1. My _____ garden was filled with _____ cactus.

2. The neighbor's _____ dog chewed up my _____ shoes. I was so mad.

3. My grandmother's _____ jewelry box if full of _____ jewelry.

4. My _____ closet is filled with _____ tennis shoes.

Look at the illustrations. Write a descriptive sentence using adjectives for each illustration.

_____   _____

_____   _____

Overview Adverbs

Directions and Sample Answers for Activity Pages

Day 1	See "Provide a Real-World Example" below.
Day 2	Read the title and directions aloud. Ask students to read the sentences and then fill in the blanks with a specific type of adverb. Have students share their sentences with a partner. Finally, have students choose one sentence and rewrite it using different adverbs.
Day 3	Read the title and directions aloud. Invite students to sort words by adverb type: how, when, where, and how often. (Answers: how—bravely, honestly, wisely, noisily; when—then, during, next, recently; where—anywhere, nowhere, here; how often—always, sometimes, usually, never) Finally, have students write four sentences using adverbs. Students should include at least one adverb in each sentence. Have students share their sentences with a partner.
Day 4	Read the title and directions aloud. Have student pairs write an **-ly** adverb that describes each illustration and write it on the line. Allow students who struggle to refer to the Day 1 Adverb Examples chart. Then have students choose two illustrations and write sentences. (Possible answers: 1—hungrily; 2—victoriously; 3—recklessly; 4—nervously)
Day 5	Read the directions aloud. Allow time for students to complete the first task. (Answers: 1—firmly; 2—finally; 3—inside; 4—frequently) Next, have students complete the second task. (Possible answer: Our cat went upstairs and slowly scratched the carpet.) Afterward, meet individually with students. Ask students to share responses with you. Discuss their results. Use their responses to plan further instruction.

Provide a Real-World Example

◆ Hand out Day 1 activity page. **Say:** *Authors want their writing to be interesting. Authors want to be clear about how, when, where, and how often things are done. Using adverbs is one way to do this. Adverbs tell more about verbs, adjectives, and other adverbs. They explain how, when, where, and how often something happens. Look at the chart on your hand out.* Have students look at the adverb chart on the hand out. Discuss four different types of adverbs.

◆ **Say:** *Now let's use the different kinds of adverbs to add life to dull sentences. Look at the first sentence.*

◆ **Say:** *This sentence doesn't tell much about me planting a garden. I think I can add an adverb, or two, to this sentence. The adverbs will give the reader more information. First, I'll tell how I planted the garden. Maybe I wanted to get the job done carefully. Carefully tells how I planted. It means I took my time and tried to make good decisions. Most adverbs that tell how end in **-ly**.*

◆ **Say:** *Now, I'll tell when I planted a garden. I did it yesterday.* Revise the sentence on the board.

◆ Repeat the process with the remaining sentences. Include two adverbs for each sentence. Allow students to help choose adverbs.

Using Adverbs

I carefully planted a garden yesterday.

I rarely run down that path.

Our dog barks loudly before someone knocks on the door.

I often played in the attic.

Name _____

Adverbs

Rewrite the sentence to include adverbs.

I planted a garden.

_____

_____

_____

Our dog barks.

_____

_____

_____

I run.

_____

_____

_____

I played.

_____

_____

_____

Adverb Examples

how	when	where	how often
carefully, nervously, recklessly, lazily, obediently, playfully, sharply, victoriously, hungrily	when, before, already, yesterday, recently, finally, just, soon, later	abroad, underground, up, upstairs, down, home, there, outside	every, never, often, rarely, frequently

Using Adverbs

**Review the Adverb Examples Chart from Day 1. Now read the sentences.
Fill in the blanks with the specific type of adverb, but do not use the same
adverb more than one time. You may choose adverbs that are not on the list.
Share your sentences with a partner.**

1. The little boy _____ returned to his mother. (**how adverb**)

2. Please come back _____ and visit. (**when adverb**)

3. I like to travel _____ in the winter. (**where adverb**)

4. I visit that store _____ time I'm in town. (**how often adverb**)

5. "Don't touch that cactus," my mom said _____ . (**how adverb**)

6. But I _____ did my homework. (**when adverb**)

7. I think I left my glasses over _____ . (**where adverb**)

8. How _____ do you go to the museum? (**how often adverb**)

**Choose one sentence and rewrite it using other adverbs.
How many different adverbs can you use for one sentence?**

_____

_____

_____

_____

Adverb Sort

Read the adverbs. Sort them by type. Share your results with a partner.

here	wisely	usually	noisily	then
bravely	next	during	honestly	recently
anywhere	never	nowhere	always	sometimes

Adverbs

how	when	where	how often

Write four sentences using adverbs. Include at least one adverb in each sentence. Share your sentences with your partner.

_____

_____

_____

_____

_____

-ly Adverbs

Look at the pictures. Talk about them with a partner. Think of an -ly adverb that describes each picture. Write the adverb on the line. Do not use the same adverb more than once.

_____

_____

_____

_____

Choose two pictures and write a sentence for each one.
Be sure to include your adverb. Share your sentences with your partner.

_____

_____

_____

Assessment

Read the sentences. Then choose an adverb from the word bank and write it on the line.

finally	frequently	firmly	inside

1. I _____ told John Jr. that he could not have a new toy.
   (how adverb)

2. We _____ got to watch TV.
   (when adverb)

3. You need to go _____ .
   (where adverb)

4. We _____ attend the movies.
   (how often adverb)

Read the sentence. Revise the sentence to include where and how often adverbs. Use the Adverb Examples Chart if necessary.

Our cat scratched the carpet.

_____

_____

Overview Strong Verbs

Directions and Sample Answers for Activity Pages

Day 1	See "Provide a Real-World Example" below.
Day 2	Read the title and directions aloud. Have students act out sentence pairs and decide which sentence contains the strong verb. Ask students to circle the sentence containing the strong verb. (Answers: 1. scurried; 2. slither; 3. giggling; 4. nibble; 5. bolt) Finally, have pairs choose one strong verb sentence to act out during whole-class time. Ask the class to identify which sentence the pair acts out.
Day 3	Read the title and directions aloud. Ask students to choose the "noun" verb that best completes each sentence and write it on the line. Have students share their answers with a partner. (Answers: 1. skunked; 2. table; 3. bubble-wrapped; 4. doctor; 5. Police; 6. snaked) Have students choose two "noun" verbs from the bank and use them in two new sentences. Ask students to share their sentences with a partner.
Day 4	Read the title and directions aloud. (Answers: 1. Jane owns the coffee shop. 2. The refinery employs one hundred people. 3. Ellen scoured the rabbit cage. 4. The Wilsons reside on Cherry Lane.) Have students read the sentences and revise them by replacing "to be" verbs with strong verbs. (Answers: 1. Everyone complained about the heat. 2. We sailed at the lake.)
Day 5	Read the directions aloud. Allow time for students to complete each task. (Answers: 1. shattered; 2. chop; 3. observed) (1. My family argued over which game to play.; 2. The dolphins leaped out of the water.) Afterward, meet individually with students to discuss their results. Use their responses to plan further instruction.

Provide a Real-World Example

◆ Hand out the Day 1 activity page. **Say:** *The English language is filled with action words. Action words are called verbs. When we write, we want to use the verb that best describes what is happening. The best verb helps the reader "see" what is happening. Look at the sentence. There is nothing wrong with the word **looked**, but it is a common word. Watch as I rewrite the sentence.* (Revise the sentence with the verb as shown here and allow students to analyze.)

◆ **Ask:** *Now this sentence gives me a clearer picture of what happened. The verb **gaze** gives a whole new meaning to the sentence. Verbs like **gaze** are called strong verbs because they create a picture in the reader's mind.*

◆ Repeat the process with the remaining sentences. Then call their attention to the chart.

◆ **Say:** *"To be" and "to have" verbs do not make sentences strong. They make weak sentences. When writing, avoid using these verbs when you can and instead think of other, more descriptive verbs.*

◆ Repeat the process with the remaining sentences.

◆ **Say:** *Remember strong verbs really show readers what is happening. Use strong verbs when you write.*

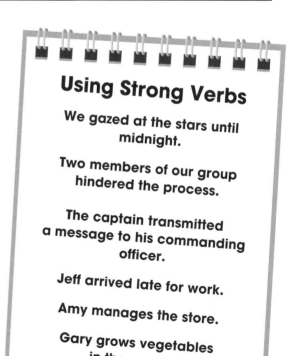

Using Strong Verbs

We gazed at the stars until midnight.

Two members of our group hindered the process.

The captain transmitted a message to his commanding officer.

Jeff arrived late for work.

Amy manages the store.

Gary grows vegetables in the garden.

Strong Verbs

Rewrite the sentences to include strong verbs.

1. We looked at the stars until midnight.

_____

_____

2. Two members of our group slowed down the process.

_____

_____

3. The captain sent a message to his commanding officer.

_____

_____

"To be" and "to have" verbs can weaken sentences.					
am	**is**	**are**	**was**	**were**	**be**
being	**been**	**have**	**having**	**has**	**had**

1. Jeff was late for work. _____

_____

2. Amy is the manager of the store. _____

_____

3. Gary has vegetables in the garden. _____

_____

Act It Out

Read each sentence pair. Act out each sentence and decide which one has the strong verb in it. Circle the sentence with the strong verb.

1. The squirrels scurried around the tree.

   The squirrels went around the tree.

2. I had to go under the house to find my ball.

   I had to slither under the house to find my ball.

3. The girls were giggling about something.

   The girls were laughing about something.

4. I turned the corner just in time to see the mouse eat a piece of cheese.

   I turned the corner just in time to see the mouse nibble a piece of cheese.

5. Close the door so the snow won't come inside the house.

   Bolt the door so the snow won't come inside the house.

Choose one strong verb sentence and act it out for the group. Have the class identify which sentence you chose.

"Noun" Verbs?

Many nouns can be transformed into strong verbs. Have you ever seen someone worm their way through a crowd? That's just what the person looks like . . . a worm. But in this case the noun "worm" is used as a verb.

Read the "noun" verbs in the word bank and the sentences that follow. Choose the best "noun" verb to complete each sentence. Share your sentences with a partner.

doctor	table	skunked	police	snaked	bubble-wrapped

We _____ our opponent 42–0.

Let's _____ this discussion until tomorrow.

My mother _____ the package before mailing it.

"I need to _____ this cat's leg," muttered the old woman.

_____ the area, and keep an eye out for anything strange.

Our plumber _____ his way through the pipes using a wire.

Choose two "noun" verbs from the bank and use them in new sentences. Share your sentences with a partner.

_____

_____

_____

_____

Avoiding "To Be" and "To Have" Sentences

Read the "to be" or "to have" verb sentences on the left side of the page. Then read the strong verb sentences on the right side of the page. Draw lines matching the sentences.

"To Be/To Have" Sentences	**Strong Verb Sentences**
1. Jane has a coffee shop.	Ellen scours the rabbit cage.
2. The refinery has one hundred employees.	Jane owns a coffee shop.
3. Ellen is a good cleaner of the rabbit cage.	The Wilsons reside on Cherry Lane.
4. The Wilsons are on Cherry Lane.	The refinery employs one hundred people.

Read the sentences. Revise them by replacing "to be" verbs with strong verbs. Share your new sentences with a partner.

1. Everyone had complaints about the heat.

_____

_____

2. We went in a sailboat at the lake.

_____

_____

Assessment

Read each sentence. Replace the underlined common verbs with strong verbs from the word bank. Rewrite each sentence on the lines provided.

observed	shattered	chop

The vase <u>broke</u> into a million pieces. _____

_____

Take the ax and <u>cut</u> down the smaller oak trees. _____

_____

She <u>watched</u> the snake slither in the grass. _____

_____

Read the sentences. Revise them by replacing the "to be" verbs with strong verbs. Share your new sentences with a partner.

1. My family had a fight about which game to play. _____

_____

2. The dolphins were up, out of the water. _____

_____

Overview   Advanced Nouns

Directions and Sample Answers for Activity Pages

Day 1	See "Provide a Real-World Example" below.
Day 2	Read the title and directions aloud. Have students share responses with a partner. Finally, have students choose three advanced nouns and use them in sentences. (Answers: girl-maiden; reason-motive; order-rank; plain-natural; teacher-instructor; cure-remedy; cost-price; spot-blemish)
Day 3	Read the title and directions aloud. (Answers: idea—notion, belief, thought; example—sample, specimen, illustration; friend—ally, partner, companion; group—clump, cluster, collection; problem—dilemma, difficulty, predicament) Finally, have students choose four nouns and write a sentence for each noun.
Day 4	Read the title and directions aloud. Ask students to draw lines matching animals on the left side with their group names on the right side. (Answers: herd of elk, gaggle of geese, flight of swans, prickle of porcupines, pack of mules, band of coyotes, tower of giraffes, swarm of ants) Have students choose three animals and their group names and use each in a sentence.
Day 5	Read the directions aloud. Allow time for students to complete each task. (Answers: clothes-garments; truth-fact; gift-donations; dream-illusion) Afterward, meet individually with students to discuss their results. Use their responses to plan further instruction.

Provide a Real-World Example

◆ Hand out the Day 1 activity page. **Ask:** *What is a noun?* (Allow responses.) **Say:** *Yes. A noun is a person, place, thing, or idea. What are some person nouns?* (Allow responses.) If students struggle, suggest nouns from the chart shown. Repeat with other noun types.

◆ Write "I have a problem." on the board. Underline **problem**. **Say:** *Authors use nouns in their writing, but good authors want to use the noun that tells exactly what they are thinking. Let's think about how to use the best noun. Look at the sentence. The word **problem** is a great noun. When I say the word **problem**, you might think of problems that you've gotten into, but I really want to use a noun that is not so common. I want to use another word, or a synonym, for **problem**. I like the word **predicament**. Watch as I revise this sentence.*

◆ Write the following revised sentence on the board: "I have a predicament." Underline **predicament**.

◆ **Say:** *Now look at the sentence. I changed **problem** to **predicament**. This sentence says what I really mean. Predicament definitely means something that needs to be resolved, but it also suggests that the problem is not a big one. If you can't think of a word to replace the common word, try using a thesaurus.* (Repeat the process with the remaining sentences using stronger nouns like **salary**, **twine**, or **clusters**.)

◆ **Say:** *Remember, authors choose words that tell exactly what they feel. Think about what you really want to say and use the best words to say it. In this unit, you will learn some of the best words to use in your writing.*

Nouns

person	place	thing	idea
people	hospital	tigers	love
nurse	house	forests	peace
brother	shop	river	belief
neighbor	living room	bicycle	honesty

Advanced Nouns

Complete the chart.

Nouns

person	place	thing	idea

Rewrite the sentences using different nouns.

I have a problem.

_____

_____

Did you get your money?

_____

_____

Tie the turkey legs with string.

_____

_____

Look at the chickens standing in groups.

_____

_____

Noun Match

Draw lines matching common nouns to more advanced nouns.
Share your thinking with a partner. Use a dictionary to define words that you do not know.

Common Nouns	**Advanced Nouns**
girl	natural
reason	blemish
order	instructor
plain	remedy
teacher	price
cure	motive
cost	rank
spot	maiden

Choose three advanced nouns and write a sentence for each.

_____

_____

_____

_____

_____

Noun Sort

Read the nouns in the word bank. Sort the nouns into the categories shown on the chart. Share your thinking with a partner. Use a dictionary to define words that you do not know.

collection	dilemma	notion	specimen	companion
thought	ally	clump	difficulty	sample
partner	belief	illustration	cluster	predicament

Noun Sort

idea	example	friend	group	problem

Choose four nouns and write a sentence for each.

_____

_____

_____

_____

Animal Groups

A troop of kangaroos? A leep of leopards? Have you ever heard of these things? They are nouns that are used for animal groups. Draw lines matching animals to their group names. Use a dictionary or the internet if needed.

Animals	Groups
elk	band
geese	swarm
swans	tower
porcupines	herd
mules	prickle
coyotes	pack
giraffes	gaggle
ants	flight

Choose three animals and their group name. Write a sentence for each.

_____

_____

_____

_____

Name _____

Assessment

Read the nouns on both sides of the paper. Draw lines matching common nouns on the left side to advanced nouns on the right.

Common Nouns	Advanced Nouns
clothes	donations
truth	fact
gift	illusion
dream	garments

Use each advanced noun in a sentence.

_____

_____

_____

_____

_____

_____

_____

Overview   Idioms

Directions and Sample Answers for Activity Pages

Day 1	See "Provide a Real-World Example" below.
Day 2	Read the title and directions aloud. (Answers: 1. I'm in a pickle. 2. That strikes me funny.; 3. The fat's in the fire. 4. I've hit the nail right on the head. 5. Her bark is worse than her bite. 6. I think I bet on the wrong horse. 7. The buck stops with me. 8. I think I bit off more than I can chew.) Finally, ask students to choose two idiom sentences and illustrate them. Then ask a partner to identify which sentences were drawn.
Day 3	Read the title and directions aloud. (Answers: 1. someone who acts like they are better than other people; 2. the boy is clumsy and could break something; 3. looking into things can be dangerous; 4. build your self-confidence)
Day 4	Read the title and directions aloud. (Answer: 1. under the weather; 2. pull their own weight; 3. pay through the nose; 4. storm in a teacup; 5. get out of hand; 6. bang your head against a wall; 7. throw in the towel; 8. make ends meet) Finally, have students choose four idioms and use them in sentences.
Day 5	Read the directions aloud. Allow time for students to complete each task. (Answers: 1. when something is funny or odd; 2. she doesn't mean for her words to sound so harsh; 3. stated the main point; 4. makes a mess) Afterward, meet individually with students. Discuss their results and plan further instruction.

Provide a Real-World Example

◆ Hand out the Day 1 activity page. **Say:** *Authors want their writing to be interesting. They want to create pictures in the minds of their readers. Using idioms is one way to do this. An idiom is a way that people talk and write. What they say isn't really what they mean. You have to know the idiom to know what the meaning really is. You are going to learn idioms in this unit. Read the sentence on the board. I think I can rewrite that sentence using an idiom. I think it will be more interesting and create a picture in the reader's mind.*

◆ Revise the sentence with the example below:
I think I can fill Mary's shoes.

◆ **Say:** *Now read the first sentence. Filling Mary's shoes? Who said anything about filling shoes? I'm not really filling Mary's shoes with anything. In this sentence, the idiom means that I can do the job as well as Mary. I can fill her shoes. Let's look at a few other idioms.*

◆ Write the following sentence on the board:
I finished the test by the time the bell rang.

◆ **Ask:** *What does this sentence say?* (Allow responses.) *Yes. That's right. It says that a person finished the test on time. A nice sentence, but not very interesting. Now look at the sentence with an idiom in it.*

◆ Revise the sentence with the example below:
I finished the test in the nick of time.

◆ **Say:** *Nick of time? What does that mean? Are you going to nick time? Of course not. It means the same thing as the first sentence. It just sounds a lot more interesting.*

◆ Repeat with the examples below:
Are you too shy to speak? (cat has your tongue)
I want to have the best of everything. (live high on the hog)

◆ **Say:** *Remember to use idioms when you write. They make writing a lot of fun.*

Idiom

a common or peculiar expression that helps readers create a picture in their minds

Name _____

Idioms

Rewrite the sentences using idioms.

1. I think I can do this job as well as Mary.

_____

_____

2. I finished the test by the time the bell rang.

_____

_____

3. Are you too shy to speak?

_____

_____

4. I want to have the best of everything.

_____

_____

Name _____

Idiom Match

Read the plain sentences on the left and the idiom sentences on the right. Draw a line from the plain sentence to its matching idiom sentence. Share your results with a partner.

Plain Sentences	**Idiom Sentences**
1. I'm in an awkward situation.	The fat's in the fire.
2. That seems so funny to me.	Her bark is much worse than her bite.
3. The damage is done. What can we do about it?	I think I bet on the wrong horse.
4. I've stated the main point.	The buck stops with me.
5. She doesn't mean for her words to sound harsh.	I'm in a pickle.
6. I did not see it happening that way.	I think I bit off more than I can chew.
7. This was my fault.	I've hit the nail right on the head.
8. I think I've got more than I can handle.	That strikes me funny.

Choose two idiom sentences and draw what they look like to you. Ask a partner to choose which sentences you drew. (Example: Draw a picture of a person dressed in a pickle costume.)

What does it really mean?

Read the sentences and look at the underlined idiom phrase. Tell what each sentence really means. Then draw a picture describing each sentence. (Example for 1: Draw a picture of Jamie sitting on a horse.) Share your thinking and drawings with a partner.

1. "You need to <u>get off your high horse</u>," Ally said to Jamie. "You are no better than I am." What does the sentence really mean?

_____

_____

2. That boy is <u>a bull in a china shop.</u> What does the sentence really mean?

_____

_____

3. I don't think you should go inside that house. Remember <u>curiosity killed the cat.</u> What does the sentence really mean?

_____

_____

4. Take your time and <u>find your feet.</u> You're new at this job. What does this sentence really mean?

_____

_____

Writing with Idioms

Read the sentences and idioms in the bank. Which idiom would you use for each sentence? Choose an idiom from the bank and write it on the line. Share your answers with a partner.

bang your head against a wall	under the weather	get out of hand	pay through the nose
pull their own weight	throw in the towel	make ends meet	storm in a teacup

1. I don't feel well. _____

2. Everyone must complete their work. _____

3. I paid a lot of money for my new car. _____

4. My sister worries about little things. _____

5. Make sure the kids behave. _____

6. This math problem is frustrating. _____

7. I quit. _____

8. The peasant could not buy bread. _____

Choose four idioms from the bank and use them in your own sentences.

_____

_____

_____

_____

Assessment

Read the sentences and look at the underlined idiom phrase.
Tell what each sentence really means.

1. That picture <u>strikes me funny.</u>

   _____

   _____

2. Don't worry. Sarah's <u>bark is worse than her bite.</u>

   _____

   _____

3. You <u>hit the nail on the head.</u>

   _____

   _____

4. Jeffrey is like <u>a bull in a china shop.</u> Nothing is safe.

   _____

   _____

Choose two idioms from the sentences above or choose two that
we've studied this week. Use them in sentences.

Overview Similes

Directions and Sample Answers for Activity Pages

Day 1	See "Provide a Real-World Example" below.
Day 2	Read the title and directions aloud. (Answers: 1. I want to soar like an eagle above the clouds. 2. Leslie is as timid as a rabbit. 3. Mr. Johnson is as old as the hills. 4. Soldiers are as tough as nails. 5. Janet eats like a bird. 6. My hands are like ice.) Have students choose two sentences from the right side, tell what is being compared, and illustrate them. Have students share their thinking and illustrations with a partner.
Day 3	Read the title and directions aloud. Have students share their work with a partner. (Answers: 1. my little sister and a bug in a rug—the little girl slept comfortably; 2. the second gymnast and a fish out of water—the second gymnast did not look like she knew what she was doing; 3. me and a daisy—I woke up feeling rested; 4. my dad and a bear in the morning—dad came home from work in a bad mood; 5. Dan's face and a cooked lobster—Dan's face was sunburned)
Day 4	Read the title and directions aloud. Ask students to review the sorts and write sentences using a simile from each category.
Day 5	Read the directions aloud. Allow time for students to complete each task. (Answers: 1. Tim and the way a bird eats—Tim does not eat very much; 2. Mrs. Kane and an old, wise owl—Mrs. Kane is very smart and should be respected; 3. My grandparents and dirt—grandparents were not just poor, they were extremely poor; 4. bikers and clouds—the bikers didn't have a home base or central location) Afterward, meet individually with students to discuss their results. Use their responses to plan further instruction.

Provide a Real-World Example

◆ Hand out the Day 1 activity page. **Say:** *Authors want their writing to be interesting. They want to create pictures in the minds of their readers. Using similes is one way to do this. A simile compares two things using the words **as** or **like**. Read the first sentence. I think I can rewrite that sentence using a simile with **as**. I think it will be more interesting and create a picture in the reader's mind.*

◆ Revise the sentence with the example shown.

◆ **Say:** *Now read the sentence. I compared my teacher to a wise, old owl using the word **as**. I'm still saying that my teacher is smart. But now, I'm saying it in a more colorful, interesting way. People have always considered older owls to be wise . . . partly because they live so long. You have to be wise to live long in the wild. Draw a picture of a teacher who looks like a wise, old owl.* (Allow time for students to draw and share.)

◆ Repeat with remaining examples. Each time **ask:** *What did I compare? Why? How does this add to my writing? How does it add to the reader's experience.* (Allow responses.)

◆ **Say:** *Similes create interesting pictures in the reader's mind. Be sure to include similes when you write.*

Simile
a comparison using
like or *as*

My teacher is as smart as an owl.

The sun hit the water and made it sparkle like diamonds.

Similes

Rewrite the sentences to include similes. Tell what is being compared.
Then draw a picture showing what the sentence is telling you.

My teacher is smart.

What is being compared?

_____

_____

The sun hit the water and made it look bright.

What is being compared?

_____

_____

Simile Match

Read the sentences in both columns. Sentences on the left do not have similes. Sentences on the right mean the same thing but have similes. Draw a line from the sentence on the left to its matching sentence on the right.

1. I want to fly high in the sky.

Janet eats like a bird.

2. Leslie was very shy.

Soldiers are as tough as nails.

3. Mr. Johnson is very old.

My hands are like ice.

4. Soldiers can handle a lot.

I want to soar like an eagle above the clouds.

5. Janet doesn't eat very much.

Leslie is as timid as a rabbit.

6. My hands were very cold.

Mr. Johnson is as old as the hills.

Choose two sentences from the right side. Tell what two things are being compared. Draw a picture showing what the sentence really means.

Picture This

Read the sentences. Under each sentence, tell what is being compared.
Then explain what the sentence means. Share your thinking with a partner.

1. **My little sister slept as snug as a bug in a rug.**

   What is being compared? _____

   What does the sentence really mean? _____

   _____

2. **The first gymnast was great, but the second one looked like a fish out of water.**

   What is being compared? _____

   What does the sentence really mean? _____

   _____

3. **I woke up feeling as fresh as a daisy.**

   What is being compared? _____

   What does the sentence really mean? _____

   _____

4. **My dad came home from work grumbling like a bear in the morning . . . and it**
   was in the afternoon.

   What is being compared? _____

   What does the sentence really mean? _____

   _____

5. **Dan spent too much time in the sun. His face looked like a freshly boiled lobster.**

   What is being compared? _____

   What does the sentence really mean? _____

   _____

Simile Sort

Authors use similes to express meaning, but they don't use just any simile. They take time to match the simile to the topic. An author writing a story with a farm setting might have an introduction like:

> **We lived on a farm not far from Raleigh, North Carolina.**
> **Behind the house, hills rolled away like sleeping giants.**

Notice how the author compared the hills to sleeping giants using the word "like." You can really see huge rolling hills behind the house. You can even pretend that they are sleeping giants.

Sort the similes in the word bank. Share your thinking with a partner.

dry as dust	old as time	drifting like clouds	flashed like a shooting star
light as air	solid as a rock	shined like the moon	big as life

Time and History	Land and Earth	Moon and Stars	Sky and Air

Review your sorts. Write a sentence using a simile from each of the four categories.

_____

_____

_____

_____

_____

Assessment

Read the sentences. Under each sentence, tell what is being compared.
Then tell what the sentence really means.

1. **Tim will never gain weight. He eats like a bird.**

    What is being compared? _____

    What does the sentence mean? _____

    _____

2. **You need to listen to Mrs. Kane. She's as wise as an old owl.**

    What is being compared? _____

    What does the sentence mean? _____

    _____

3. **My grandparents lived through the Great Depression. They were as poor as dirt.**

    What is being compared? _____

    What does the sentence mean? _____

    _____

4. **The bikers were like drifting clouds. They just wanted to travel.**

    What is being compared? _____

    What does the sentence mean? _____

    _____

Overview Metaphors

Directions and Sample Answers for Activity Pages

Day 1	See "Provide a Real-World Example" below.
Day 2	Read the title and directions aloud. Have students share thinking with a partner. (Answers: 1. woolly mammoth and ice—the woolly mammoth was found in a block of ice; 2. the president's heart and a stone—the president did not care what happened to his employees; 3. the ice cream cone and a light—the ice cream cone made the person feel much better after a hard day; 4. the garden and a forest—the garden was overgrown with weeds)
Day 3	Read the title and directions aloud. Have students share their thinking and drawings with a partner. (Answers: 1. the sentence means that the toys reminded the person of his past; 2. the sentence means that the sleet came down quickly and would hurt if it hit someone; 3. the sentence means that the graduate was young but was ready to go out into life and grow; 4. the sentence means that the fox family liked the comfortable cold air)
Day 4	Read the title and directions aloud. Ask students to sort metaphors into four categories. Ask students to review the sorts and write sentences using a metaphor from each category.
Day 5	Read the directions aloud. Allow time for students to complete each task. (Answers: 1. principal and a stone—the principal does not care about the students; 2. backyard and forest—the backyard was overgrown with weeds; 3. classroom and furnace—the classroom was very hot; 4. car and a refrigerator—the car was very cold) Afterward, meet individually with students to discuss their results. Use their responses to plan further instruction.

Provide a Real-World Example

◆ Hand out the Day 1 activity page. **Say:** *Authors want to create pictures in the minds of their readers. Using metaphors is one way to do this. A metaphor compares two things. Metaphors do not use **like** or **as** like similes do. Read the sentence on the board. I think I can rewrite that sentence using a metaphor. I think it will be more interesting and create a picture in the reader's mind.* Revise the sentence with the example shown.

◆ **Say:** *Now read the sentence. I compared the photo album with history that has been forgotten. I'm still saying that the photo album contains old pictures, but now I'm including the emotional side of it. Photo albums remind us of our history . . . many times, history long forgotten. You may even be able to draw a picture in your mind of a photo album with a pop-up picture that shows an event from your past. Can you see that? Try drawing that picture on your hand out.*

◆ Allow time for students to draw and share artwork with the class. Then repeat with remaining examples.

◆ **Say:** *Do you see how a metaphor made you think in a different way. Metaphors create those interesting pictures in the reader's mind. Be sure to include metaphors when you write.*

Metaphor

A comparison without using like or as

The photo album was a journey through time.

When my mom canned pickles, the kitchen was a furnace.

Metaphors

Rewrite the sentences to include metaphors. Tell what is being compared. Then draw a picture showing what the sentence is telling you.

The photo album had old pictures in it.

_____

_____

When my mom canned pickles, the kitchen was hot.

_____

_____

What Does This Mean?

Read the sentences. Tell what is being compared. Then explain
what the sentence is really telling you. Share your thinking with a partner.

1. **The woolly mammoth found in Asia was frozen in time.**

    What is being compared? _____

    What does the sentence really mean? _____

    _____

2. **The company's president has a heart of stone.**

    What is being compared? _____

    What does the sentence really mean? _____

    _____

3. **I'd had a rough day. Though it may sound corny, the ice cream cone was a**
    light in a sea of darkness.

    What is being compared? _____

    What does the sentence really mean? _____

    _____

4. **After months of neglect, the garden was a forest.**

    What is being compared? _____

    What does the sentence really mean? _____

    _____

Picture This

Read the sentences. Draw a picture showing what the sentence sounds like to you. Then explain what the sentence really means. Share your thinking and drawings with a partner.

Example: **That boy is a pig.**

The sentence really means that the boy is messy.

1. I found a box of toys under my bed. They were a bridge to my past.

What does the second sentence really mean?

_____

2. The sleet came down in sharp tacks.

What does the sentence really mean?

_____

3. "You're a seed ready to sprout," the mother said to her high school graduate.

What does the sentence really mean?

_____

4. The fox family thought the wintry cold air was a smooth blanket of comfort.

What does the sentence really mean?

_____

Metaphor Sort

Authors use metaphors to express meaning, but they don't use just any metaphor. They take time to match the metaphor to the topic. An author writing a story might have an introduction like:

> **Growing up, we lived in a huge house in northern Louisiana. Our backyard was an island overgrown with weeds. Neighbors? Well, we knew we had them, but we couldn't see their houses for all the leaves.**

Notice how the author compared the backyard to an island overgrown with weeds. The author suggests that the vines were so thick that he couldn't see his neighbor's yard. It was as if his family lived all alone on an island.

Sort the metaphors in the bank. Share your thinking with a partner.

center of the universe	cloud of confusion	sea of sand	a bridge to the past
island of overgrown weeds	pockets of cold air	frozen in time	tapestry of stars

Time and History	Land and Earth	Moon and Stars	Sky and Air

Review your sorts. Write a sentence using a metaphor from each of the four categories.

_____

_____

_____

Assessment

**Read the sentences. Under each sentence, tell what is being compared.
Then tell what the sentence really means.**

1. **Our principal has a heart of stone.**

    What is being compared? _____

    What does the sentence mean? _____

    _____

2. **When we returned from our vacation, we found that our backyard was a forest.**

    What is being compared? _____

    What does the sentence mean? _____

    _____

3. **Our classroom was a furnace.**

    What is being compared? _____

    What does the sentence mean? _____

    _____

4. **The car was a refrigerator.**

    What is being compared? _____

    What does the sentence mean? _____

    _____

Overview   Object Personification

Directions and Sample Answers for Activity Pages

Day 1	See "Provide a Real-World Example" below.
Day 2	Read the title and directions aloud. (Answers: 1. Rain kissed my cheeks as it fell. 2. The green strawberries said, "Don't eat me yet." 3. The oven timer said my dinner was ready. 4. Stars danced in the night sky. 5. The sun played hide and seek with me. 6. My motorcycle coughed when I tried to start it.) Have students choose two sentences from the right side and illustrate them. Have students share their illustrations with a partner.
Day 3	Read the title and directions aloud. Have students share their thinking and drawings with a partner. (Answers: 1. leaves covered everything in the city; 2. the sun shone into someone's bedroom; 3. it didn't rain very much; 4. the jack-o-lantern had a smile cut into its face)
Day 4	Read the title and directions aloud. (Answers: 1. the mother blinked her lights off and on; 2. the bed creaked from age. 3. the wind bent the trees; 4. there was a lot of lightning) Finally, ask students to get in pairs and act out the sentences.
Day 5	Read the directions aloud. Allow time for students to complete each task. (Answers: 1. the stars seemed to sparkle; 2. it stormed all night with lots of lightning and thunder; 3. the dull-colored winter backyard became bright with spring colors; 4. the grass needed watering) Afterward, meet individually with students to discuss their results. Use their responses to plan further instruction.

Provide a Real-World Example

◆ Hand out the Day 1 activity page. **Say:** *Authors want their writing to be interesting. They want to create pictures in the minds of their readers. Using personification is one way to do this. Personification gives human traits to inhuman, or inanimate, objects. In other words, personification gives life to objects. Read the sentence on the board. I think I can revise that sentence using personification. I think it will be more interesting and create a picture in the reader's mind.*

◆ Revise the sentence with the examples shown.

◆ **Say:** *Now read the sentence. Flowers are not human. They cannot talk and they certainly can't ask for water. But by using personification, I turned a boring sentence into something with life. You may even be able to draw a picture of the wilting flower begging for water, kind of like a cartoon. Try drawing a begging, wilted flower on your handout.*

◆ Allow time for students to draw and share their artwork with the class.

◆ **Say:** *Do you see how giving human qualities to non-human things adds "life" to writing? It creates those interesting pictures in the reader's mind. Be sure to include personification when you write.*

Personification

The flower wilted in the sun, it begged for water.

The wind howled as it raced around the house.

Personification

Rewrite the sentences to include personification. Then draw a picture showing what the sentence is telling you.

The flowers wilted in the hot sun. They needed water.

_____

_____

The wind was loud.

_____

_____

Personification Match

Read the sentences in both columns. Draw a line from the sentence on the left to its matching sentence on the right.

1. Rain fell on my cheeks.

2. The green strawberries were not ready to eat.

3. The oven timer buzzed.

4. The stars looked like they were moving.

5. Clouds moved over the sun.

6. My motorcycle would not start.

The oven timer said my dinner was ready.

My motorcycle coughed when I tried to start it.

Stars danced in the night sky.

The sun played hide and seek with me.

Rain kissed my cheeks as it fell.

The green strawberries said, "Don't eat me yet."

Choose two sentences from the right side. Draw pictures illustrating the sentences.

Example: The headlights winked at me.

Picture This

Read the sentences. Draw a picture showing what the sentence sounds like to you. Then explain what the sentence really means. Share your thinking and drawings with a partner.

Example: **The radio jumped to life when I turned it on.**
The sentence really means that the radio played music
when it was turned on.

1. **Leaves wrapped a brown blanket
   over the city.**

   What does the sentence really mean?

   _____

   _____

2. **The sun said, "Hello, sleepyhead.
   Time to wake up."**

   What does the sentence really mean?

   _____

   _____

3. **Raindrops tiptoed around our house.**

   What does the sentence really mean?

   _____

   _____

4. **The jack-o-lantern smiled at me.**

   What does the sentence really mean?

   _____

   _____

What Does This Mean?

Read the sentences. Explain what the sentence means. Share your thinking with a partner.

1. **The headlights of my mom's car winked at me as I drove past her. I was in trouble.**

   What does the first sentence mean?

   _____

   _____

2. **My bed groaned when I crawled into it. I think I need a new mattress.**

   What does the first sentence mean?

   _____

   _____

3. **Trees honored the wind by bowing down.**

   What does the sentence mean?

   _____

   _____

4. **Lightning danced across the sky.**

   What does the sentence mean?

   _____

   _____

Reread each sentence. With a partner, act out what the sentence sounds like to you.

Assessment

Read the sentences. Tell what each sentence really means.

1. The stars winked at me.

   _____

   _____

2. Lightning and thunder argued all night long.

   _____

   _____

3. Color jumped into our backyard once Spring arrived.

   _____

   _____

4. The grass begged for water.

   _____

   _____

Overview Varying Sentence Structure

Directions and Sample Answers for Activity Pages

Day 1	See "Provide a Real-World Example" below.
Day 2	Read the title and directions aloud. (Possible answers: 1. Saturday, I ate pizza and went to Aunt Sally's house. 2. No one knew why the pretzels were all over the floor. 3. James was sick with the flu so he went to the doctor. 4. A hurricane hit Galveston and knocked out power to most of the island.)
Day 3	Read the title and directions aloud. (Answers: 1. Our neighbors moved into a new house in New York City. 2. I love chocolate doughnuts with sprinkles.;3. The football team played their rival and won the game 28–21. 4. I want a tree house decorated with flowers. 5. School is fun and exciting because we do different things.) Finally, ask students to illustrate one sentence.
Day 4	Read the title and directions aloud. If students struggle, have them review sentences from Day 3. (Possible answers: 1. David tripped over a toy because he wasn't paying attention. 2. Tom read a poem at school and did a great job. 3. The girls are playing in their bedroom. 4. Ellen didn't get out of bed so she was late to school and got in trouble.) Finally, ask students to choose one combined sentence and illustrate it.
Day 5	Read the directions aloud. (Possible answers: 1. The toy stopped because the batteries ran out.; 2. We bought ice from the store because our ice maker broke last night.; 1. Our cat had four kittens this morning. 2. Snow covers the gorgeous mountain peaks.) Afterward, meet individually with students to discuss their results and plan further instruction.

Provide a Real-World Example

◆ Hand out the Day 1 activity page. After students read the paragraph **ask:** *What is this paragraph about?* (Allow responses.) *What does this paragraph tell us? This paragraph gives information about the American Revolution, but it doesn't sound very interesting. What do you notice about the sentences?* (Allow responses.)

◆ **Say:** *Yes. The sentences look alike, or similar. Almost all of them begin the same way. One way that authors make their writing interesting is to change the way their sentences look. I bet I can make this paragraph more interesting. I can do that three different ways. I can start sentences with different words. I can combine short sentences, and I can add details.* Point out the ways to change sentences in the sidebar on the hand out page.

◆ **Say:** *Watch as I rewrite this paragraph. I like the first sentence, but I think I can combine it with the second sentence.* Rewrite the first sentence as shown.

◆ **Say:** *I like the facts in the third sentence, but it seems so boring and doesn't have any details. Watch how I revise it and include the fourth sentence in my revisions.*

◆ **Say:** *I like the last sentence, but I think I can revise it to make it better.*

◆ Have a student read the revised paragraph. Have students copy the revised paragraph on their handout or try revising it themselves.

◆ **Say:** *Now look at my paragraph. It's longer, but it also sounds better and says more about the American Revolution. I combined sentences, added details, and I started each sentence with different words. Remember to vary your sentences when you write.*

Varying Sentence Structure

The American Revolution was a famous war fought in the late 1700s. It was a war about a very simple idea . . . freedom. Americans wanted to govern themselves and England wanted to maintain control. After many years and lots of bloodshed, America won its freedom from England. The world would never be the same.

Varying Sentence Structure

Rewrite the paragraph.

The American Revolution was a war. The American Revolution was fought in the late 1700s. The American Revolution was fought between the English and the Americans. The American Revolution was about freedom. The Americans won their freedom.

_____

_____

_____

_____

_____

_____

_____

_____

_____

_____

Add Detail

Read each sentence. Read the questions after each sentence.
Write a new sentence that answers both questions.

1. **I ate pizza.** (When did you eat pizza? Where did you eat pizza?)

_____

_____

2. **No one knew why.** (What did no one know about?)

_____

_____

3. **James was sick.** (Why was James sick? What did James do because he was sick?)

_____

_____

4. **A hurricane hit.** (Where did the hurricane hit? What happened because of the hurricane?)

_____

_____

Choose one sentence that you have changed. Draw a picture of the sentence.

Sentence Match-Up

Match the sentence groups to the correct sentences in the bank. Share your results with a partner.

The football team played their rival and won the game 28–21.	School is fun and exciting because we do different things.	Our neighbors moved into a new house in New York City.	I want a tree house decorated with flowers.	I love chocolate doughnuts with sprinkles.

1. Our neighbors moved to a new house. The house is in New York City.

_____

2. I love doughnuts. I like chocolate. I like sprinkles.

_____

3. The football team won. The score was 28–21. The football team played their rival.

_____

4. I want a tree house. It should be decorated with flowers.

_____

5. School is fun. School is exciting. We do different things at school.

_____

Choose one new combined sentence and draw a picture of it.

Combining Sentences

Read the sentences. Combine them into one sentence.

1. David tripped over a toy.
    David wasn't paying attention.

    _____

    _____

    _____

2. Tom read a poem.
    Tom did this at school.
    Tom sounded great.

    _____

    _____

    _____

3. The girls are in their bedroom.
    The girls are playing.

    _____

    _____

    _____

4. Ellen didn't get out of bed.
    Ellen was late for school.
    Ellen got in trouble.

    _____

    _____

    _____

Choose one new combined sentence and draw a picture of it.

```



```

Assessment

Read each sentence. Read the questions after each sentence.
Write a new sentence that answers the questions.

1. The toy stopped. (Why did it stop?)

_____

_____

_____

2. Our ice maker broke. (When did it break? What did you do about it?)

_____

_____

_____

Read the sentences. Combine them into one sentence.
Share your sentence with a partner.

1. **Our cat had kittens.**
   She had four kittens.
   She had them yesterday.

_____

_____

_____

2. **The mountains are gorgeous.**
   The mountains are peaked.
   They are covered in snow.

_____

_____

_____

Notes

Notes